The Street-wise Popular Practical Guides

"Lady Teviot has distilled over half a century's experience of family history research into this detailed yet highly approachable guide. Her style engages the reader from the outset, and succeeds in conveying a wealth of information through combining clearly-presented fact with details of her own genealogical journey, which has taken her from a beginner to a researcher with an international reputation.

"Every aspect of family history is covered, with hints and shortcuts which will smooth the beginner's path in what can be a treacherous field. And don't think this book is just for the inexperienced – I have been working with records for over 40 years and as well as enjoying some new family history anecdotes, learnt much about the record sources which some of us take for granted. You may not be a Street-wise genealogist when you embark on this book, but you certainly will be when you finish it."

– Christopher Whittick, *County Archivist, East Sussex.*

EER Street-wise Guides, No. 3.

The Street-wise Guide to Doing Your Family History

Lady Teviot

EER

Edward Everett Root, Publishers, Brighton, 2018.

Contents

I wonder if any of you can pinpoint one small thing that has altered the course of your life in a quite unexpected way? For me it was a shaft of sunlight which led me on a completely new and for the most part a very interesting and exciting path. My work in this field. History was one of my favourite subjects at school, and from the age of eleven or twelve I used to try and draw up the genealogical tables of the kings and queens, Richard the 2nd and Charles the 2nd being my favourites. I started the wrong way round, coming down from William the Conqueror, and I would get hopelessly lost after about Henry the 3rd. I wanted to find out about the princesses but they rarely got a mention in the history books. Always at the back of my mind, fixed firmly, was the resolve that I would find out about my family.

Not long after Charles and I were first married we went on a walking holiday in Yorkshire. We visited various places of interest *en route,* though not with any premeditated plan or great design. One of the places we arrived at was the Norman church of Kirby Malham. I was wandering round looking at all the things one normally looks at in old churches and suddenly a shaft of sunlight came piercing through a window and drew my eye to a memorial on the wall. In particular to where it rested on the name of Ramsden, my mother's maiden name.

It was like a thunderbolt! I felt that this was it, this was the nudge that fate had given me to get me going to fulfil that dream that laziness or procrastination had held me back from for so long. It was like Moses on Mount Sinai or Joseph dreaming of his heavenly ladder. Well, perhaps not quite like that, but it certainly gave me the impetus to get on with the job. It was rather ironic really; in having thought Ramsden was a special sort of name, I then discovered that Ramsden in Yorkshire and Lancashire is as common as Jones in Wales or Mac something or other in Scotland.

My maternal grandmother who had died long before I was born always said the Ramsdens came from Yorkshire. I was unlucky that the other three had also died before I was born. As soon as we got home I went to see my mother and collected as much information as she could give me on names and dates of births, marriages, deaths and addresses. She told me her parents were buried in a cemetery in the East of London. I was fortunate in being able to ask her 'in the living years', as it were. For time never comes back – and everyone should try to do this before it is too late.

Because of my mother's help we did not take the next logical step which was Somerset House. Instead, we went to the cemetery. Abney Park was then an overgrown and partially derelict place. It was first opened by the Lord Mayor of London in 1840 because by then the parish churchyards in London were packed to capacity and there were three Burial Acts passed in order to relieve the overcrowding. In the Victorian era death and its accompanying ceremonies played a large part in everyday life. To some the ultimate sad fate would be to have a pauper's funeral or to be buried 'on the parish'. Abney Park was typical of its kind, highly fashionable when it first opened with ornate monuments and headstones of every description. Those buried there include General William Booth, founder of the Salvation Army.

The grounds covered 32 acres and were described as well-timbered with varieties of forest trees which pleasantly shaded the many walks. But by the Second World War maintenance was minimal and the company was declared bankrupt. It is now managed by a local Trust, and you can search burial entries online. The Abney Park Cemetery was created by George Collison, the son of a Congregational Minister in 1839 (and opened in 1840) from the unconverted grounds of the Abney House and Fleetwood House estates. It succeeded Bunhill Fields as a principal nonconformist (or non-denominational) cemetery in North London while also serving as a new, hygienic public cemetery for the area. Bunhill Fields burial ground, opened in 1665, was unconsecrated, and so important dissenters, including John Bunyan, Daniel Defoe and Susanna Wesley (mother of John Wesley) were buried there. Abney Park was on unconsecrated ground, too, and with a non-denominational chapel for the dissenting community. Those buried there include the great radical publisher William Hone, in 1842, and his wife Sarah in 1864. Abney Park was part of the first wave of the formation of London's public and non-denominational cemeteries. It was planned as an informal botanical garden, and by the end of the century it had 2,500 different types of shrub, 1,000 varieties of rose and 100,000 graves. It was initially spaciously planned, but burials soon became very dense. The Abney Park Cemetery remained a public company until 1978. It was finally purchased by Hackney Borough Council for £1 in 1979. It is now preserved as a 31-acre oasis of countryside by the Abney Park Cemetery Trust, which was founded after the cemetery company went bankrupt in 1972. See www.abney-park.org.uk

Ben Wilson comments in his book *The Laughter of Triumph. William Hone and the Fight for The Free Press* (London, Faber and Faber, 2005): "The happy consequence of neglect is a thirty-one acre pocket of untamed woodland and wild flowers, rightly cherished as an unique oasis of countryside and urban sprawl. The roar of traffic from Stoke Newington High Street and Stamford Hill fades to a murmur as the visitor passes the gates, enters the dense wood and walks the narrow avenues and paths; the only sound is birdsong, and on a spring morning the scent of wild flowers and damp moss begins to penetrate petrol-enveloped nostrils."

We went to Abney Park because we knew some of my mother's family were buried there and we had heard stories of people finding family vaults and tombstones. Though in general these expeditions can be frustrating, with many of the inscriptions becoming illegible due to weather conditions and general neglect.

However, it is an important step to take for the Street-wise enquirer interested in family history.

We were lucky, as there was a little kind of lodge at the entrance gates which was the office. In there we found an aged man surrounded by great ledgers in which were the names and numbers of all the graves. Yes, he had entries for Ramsden. In fact, there were three graves and there was a space in one of them just waiting to be filled. Would we require it to be opened for the funeral, he asked, looking hopefully at us? Beating a hasty retreat, we walked up and down the paths. We found the graves of my grandparents, my great grandparents and my great, great grandfather, and we could still read the inscriptions. From them we learned that eight of my great aunts and uncles had died before they reached the age of nineteen. Later, from their death certificates, we discovered that they had all died from that terrible scourge of consumption which had no respect for age or rank. My mother remembers that her father said that he had watched his brothers and sisters sicken and die, and wondered whose turn was it next? Doubtless their illness was aggravated by those appalling pea-souper fogs which Londoners had to endure – the last of which was in 1952.

This was not a poor family. My great grandparents were comfortably off. They all lived in the gate house next to the factory which was in my mother's family for four generations from the

1830s to just after the Second World War. The factory produced a number of items for the brewery trade. In the 1892 London street directory is the following description: "Ramsden and Son Millwrights Engineers Brass and iron Founders Coppersmiths and Coopers Brewery Distillery Steam Laundry Cement Colour Petroleum Dyers Tobacco and Soda Water Machinery Turning Boring and Planing for the trade."

You name it, they made it or they did it. In 1896 they won a Gold Medal at the Brewer's Exhibition, which can't have been bad for trade. I have got rather ahead of myself, but I was so thrilled to find firm evidence about the lives of my ancestors. Now my husband, who was with me, could not quite share my enthusiasm. He could not understand why anyone should want to trace their ancestors. Of course it had always been easy for him if he wanted to check up on them all he had to do was to consult a *Burke's* or *Debrett's* and there it all was. Which sounds very nice but I think it means that people like him and H.M. The Queen miss out the thrill of the hunt of chasing up clues which all of us must do when we trace our genealogy. As he is a very patient man, he was prepared to humour me and, armed with all the information we had gleaned from the gravestones, we made our first visit to the General Register Office at Somerset House.

This was (and remains) a beautiful building on the south side of The Strand and known the world over. The galleries there then contained shelves and shelves of indexes. Red indexes for the birth entries, green indexes for the marriage indexes, and black indexes for the death entries. The indexes beginning on the 1st of July 1837 were divided into the four quarters of the year. They were mostly hand written on vellum up to 1865, and after this they were printed. They are just like telephone directories starting at A and ending at Z. I remember that I was slightly bewildered when a lady – after studying the indexes for some time – heaved a big sigh and said to herself, "Oh dear, my name can't be in there", and mournfully wandered away.

On our first visit we found what we wanted fairly quickly: my grandfather's birth entry in the September Quarter of 1850, Registration District Shoreditch. We filled in the application – coloured like the indexes, red for births, green for marriages and black for deaths. There was a gentleman searching next to us from the Church Army and we asked what we did next. He replied, "Take it to the counter and you pay. You get nought for nought here." Handing the form over, we were asked very briefly whether it was post or collect. I asked what that meant and was told I could collect it in forty-eight hours but it would take longer by post. I then asked if there was a difference in price and was told it was the princely sum of eight shillings.

Information on a certificate leads you to the next step in your research, which should be the Census returns. At that time only the 1841/51/61 were available to see. You saw the original returns then, but later they were transferred to microfilm. From the returns you can find a place of birth – although on the 1841 Census only a 'Yes' or 'No' to a county is given and without specifying the place in a county. This should lead you to the place of birth of your ancestor. The later Censuses give the full address, including the name of villages or towns where births took place. If your ancestor's birth took place overseas there are separate ledgers.

Briefly, then I got my Ramsdens back from London to Essex. The address on my grandfather's birth certificate found his father and his grandfather were in partnership running a factory in Shoreditch and the grandfather, Robert Ramsden, had been born in Hornchurch in Essex circa 1796.

Parish Registers begin in September 1538. What is certainly little short of a tragedy is how many have been lost to us. Some through carelessness, some through natural causes, some through crass stupidity and one register was nibbled at the edges by mice. However, with the information from the Census we were on our way to search the Parish Registers in the Essex Record Office in Chelmsford. There we found Robert's baptism, the son of Joseph and Alice, in 1797. We found his parents' marriage and his parents' burials. Joseph lived on until 1827 when he died aged eighty-two. It is not always straight-forward, however, to find records of baptisms. I am still looking for his baptism but one day I hope I will locate this. Local record offices hold baptism registers where they hold surviving local church records.

This seems a sort of Dick Whittington story, or possibly *Room at the Top*. A young lad, Robert Ramsden, up from the country wooed and won the daughter of his boss John Grigory in the East End of London. A little later on when his father-in-law died he inherited the factory.

Some family historians discover criminal pasts, people transported, and so forth. It is well worth searching the records for this information – and I give guidance in my bibliographical notes at the end of the book. But my ancestors were not a particularly villainous lot. Nothing very dramatic like this happened to them. Nobody hung or murdered or transported for stealing a handkerchief or poaching a rabbit. A pity about that because it is much easier to trace people who in some way broke the law. If there is somebody in your family who served in the Army or the Navy there are good records with physical descriptions given. Members of the professions can be found more easily, but so many of us come from 'ordinary' working people – listed in the records as Ag Lab (Agricultural Labourer). It is a great relief when you find a Cowman or a Shepherd.

When we started looking into the past there were not many working openings for researchers aiding others in family history. This was mostly part-time work for retired people. But after about six months of chasing my ancestors we decided that this was what we wanted to do. So we wrote offering our very amateur services to a genealogical company. To our amazement we were given a few cases to work on, and it snowballed from there.

In the Seventies Alex Haley's programme *Roots* led to tremendous interest in family history, which has grown steadily over the years. People have become hooked and it is extraordinary how it affects all ages and a very wide cross-section of society. Another important factor has been the influence of the Jesus Christ Church of Latter Day Saints – otherwise the Mormons. It is necessary for them to find their ancestors and the Church has filmed and digitised many thousands of archives to help us in our research. They run the extensive 'Ancestry.com' service, to which most libraries now subscribe. The Street-wise student who wishes to subscribe personally should watch out for the regular discount offers for this.

When you start your research my advice is that you do talk to as many of the older generation of the family as possible. How many of us now regret that we did not ask questions about the past. Why we did not listen when Uncle Albert or Great Aunt Sarah told yet again that interminable boring story about their long dead relations. I do not think either of us realised that day in Kirby Malham church how much the past would give us. Our own research business – not just for Family History but Probate Research – led to me appearing on 'Heir Hunters', to Media and Literary Research, and to speaking on my favourite subject in Australia, New Zealand, Canada, America and South Africa as well as to many organisations here at home.

In our researches we have found many tragedies in families. Many rags to riches stories, or riches to rags in three generations, and many funny entries. Two which always for me raise a smile: a churchyard inscription "In Joyous Memory of Arthur Harris who was President of the Swindon Rifle Club for twenty years. Sadly missed." And "Women Drivers: Here lies the body of Sarah White: she signalled left and then turned right."

Chapter 2: Establishing the General Register Office

The General Register office is fundamental for the Street-wise historian. Its history, and how the system was established, worked and how it changed is of great interest and provides important guidance for the successful enquirer after their ancestors. The office of Registrar General of Births, Deaths and Marriages for England and Wales was created in 1837, based in the neo-classical mansion Somerset House on the south side of The Strand in London. In 1854 there was established a Registrar General for Scotland in Edinburgh.

As early as 1753 Mr. Thomas Potter, MP for Aylesbury, Okehampton and St Germans and the second son of the Archbishop of Canterbury, had put forward a Bill for a more comprehensive and compulsory system for the registration of births and deaths, and with registers being kept with printed headings and columns for the relevant information open to all religions.

The Bill also contained suggestions for a Census of the population to be taken. Government wanted to know how many men could be called to arms and how many mouths had to be fed. This was deeply unpopular and considered to be profane and subversive of civil liberty. On the 30th of May 1753 the Bill was passed in the House of Commons but was defeated in the House of Lords. What an opportunity was missed! It would not be until 1801 that a national Census was taken. This was literally a count of heads. It was some eighty-odd years later in 1841 that Thomas Potter's idea came to fruition. It was only after the parliamentary Reform Act of 1832 that a Select Committee was appointed to look into the system of parochial registration. That is, where baptisms, burials and marriages were recorded in the Parish Registers. This Select Committee was to consider the merits of Civil Registration. The conclusion was that there should be a national system administered by a General National Office, and two Bills were introduced to achieve this: namely the Registration Act for births and deaths (which also provided for the cause of death) and the Marriage Act of 1836.

The parish clergy were to perform the registration of church marriages, and the new local Registrars were to perform all others. Marriage registration, like birth and death registration, was to be linked with a central supervisory body. Although it was spoken of as National, the new system did not include Scotland or Ireland. There was no official registration of births in Ireland before 1865. But Wales was included in 1837. King William the Fourth died on the 20th of June 1837 and the new Acts came into force on the 1st of July 1837.

Although vital for all family historians now, when Civil Registration was discussed in parliament it was not popular with certain sections of the community. Opponents of the idea included members of the clergy and the Archbishop of Canterbury himself. The clergy felt strongly that it threatened the Act of Baptism. Parents could feel that baptism was unnecessary and that they – the clergy – would be undermined. It would certainly come as a surprise to them that now there are well over 260 million registration records.

Somerset House contained among its revenue departments those for Salt, Stamp, Excise, Land Tax, Hawkers and Pedlars, Hackney Coaches and Lottery Offices. As Anthony Trollope put it, this was a nest of Public Offices. The Royal Academy had held it first exhibition there in the spring of 1780. In 1837 this was moved to Trafalgar Square and their room was to be used by the new Register Office. There it remained until the end of 1973. Some may remember the narrow galleries which by then had become very overcrowded.

One of the major questions which had to be settled before Civil Registration could be established was what local arrangements would be practicable? Should the clergy act as Civil Officers? Should the Registrar be an Elected officer, perhaps acting under the direction of a clergyman? Or should the appointments be entirely civil? If so, what should constitute a Registration District and who should appoint the Registrar? Before the reform of Local Government which would set up County Councils in 1888 no suitable local authority existed. Under the Poor Law reform Act of 1834 the Poor Law Commissioners had been appointed for Aggregates of Parishes – called Unions, hence Union Workhouses – to administer Poor Relief. It was these Unions which the 1836 Registration Act specified should form the basis of Superintendent Registrar's Districts. The Districts then being further subdivided into Sub districts for birth and death Registrations. The Act further specified that the Clerk to the Board of Guardians should have the qualifications which the Registrar General considered necessary to also become the Superintendent Registrar.

The subdivision of the areas into 619 civil registration Districts was to be determined by the local Board of Guardians, subject once again to the approval of the Registrar General. The Board of Guardians was the body which had replaced the Overseers of the Poor. They were responsible for the Administration of the Workhouses. Each member of the Board was constituted by the Poor Law Commissioners. They met weekly and were elected yearly.

From the date of his appointment in September 1836 Thomas Henry Lister the Registrar General – who was a comparatively young man, born in 1800 – set to work. In his first annual report to the Home Secretary he describes how he had sent out a series of circular letters to all the Board of Guardians. These pointed out the general principles which would determine the formation of the Districts. Included were the qualifications needed for both Superintendent Registrars and Registrars of Births and Deaths. By the end of September 1838, 2,193 Registrars had been appointed, and by the end of the year 619 Superintendent Registrars.

In the early nineteenth century, when roads and methods of transport were very different from what we know today, the size of the District or Sub District were critically important. The original Church Registration system was parochial, so informants only had to travel within the limits of the parish or the adjacent parish. When the Districts were substituted for the parish they comprised an average of seven parishes and upward. In this first Act the responsibility was placed on the Registrar, who – if he was to do his job properly – would in most cases have to travel either on foot or on horseback to the individual house where the event had taken place. More than thirty years later, the Registrar General, reviewing the working of the system in his annual report of 1872, estimated that the average area of a Sub District was twenty six and a half square miles and the average population was 10,347.

There was considerable variation between different areas. For the Poor Law Commissioners and the Board of Guardians had divided the country apparently without any very definite rule as to size or population. The Registrar General went on to note that the extremes were very wide. For example, the Sub District of Berwick Street, St. James in London comprised only 24 acres, while Bellingham in Northumberland (round the tributaries of the North Tyne) comprised 175.131 acres.

The Superintendent Registrar was responsible for examining and publishing the notices which would enable a marriage to take place. He was also the person able to celebrate, according to prescribed form, the marriages of those who only wanted a civil marriage. The arrangements for civil marriage did not affect existing arrangements whereby the Church of England (and the Church of Wales) solemnised and registered their own marriages. Nor did it affect the Society of Friends, commonly called the Quakers, or members of the Jewish community. Other religious denominations (such as the Non-Conformists) were entitled to apply for their buildings to be registered for marriage ceremonies. A Registrar of the District had to be present to register the actual marriage. By the end of 1838, 817 such Registrars had been appointed, of whom 419 were also Registrars of Births and Deaths.

Requirements to provide and equip Register Offices were made for the Superintendent Registrars, but Registrars had to provide their own accommodation. There had already been strong criticism of the choice of the Poor Law Unions as Registration Districts even before the 1836 Act was passed. The close association of the Superintendent Registrar's office with the Workhouse gave further weight to the arguments. Remuneration of the Registration Officers was by fee according to the number of entries made, for certified copies of these entries and for celebration or for attendance at marriages. Before he could grant any licence for a marriage the Superintendent Registrar also had to give security by his bond in the sum of one hundred pounds to the Registrar General for the due and faithful execution of his Office. A report in *The Times* on the 21st of September 1836 described a Meeting of the Board of Directors and Guardians of the poor of Marylebone to choose a Superintendent Registrar. To discharge the Parish duty under the acts claimed the income might be substantial. £300 per year derived from 9d. out of every shilling paid to the Registrars and the licensing and matrimonial fees by parties who shall esteem marriages a civil rather than a sacred rite. The rest of the salary would be paid out of the consolidated fund. The Registrars were paid half a crown for the first twenty entries of Births and Deaths in a calendar year and a shilling for an entry thereafter.

The substantial £300 for Superintendent Registrars was soon being questioned, partly because of the disparity in income between different types of area. Rural areas, for example, were large in size but thinly populated so yielding only a small fee income. At the beginning of 1840 the Registrar General was already writing to the Marquess of Normanby, Secretary of State for the Home Department, about the very small and inadequate amount of remuneration to Superintendent Registrars which in some cases he described as a pittance as scarcely equalled for a whole year what an agricultural labourer could earn in a fortnight. He enclosed certified copies of the amounts received in the first year of registration in 42 Districts, all under £4 and one of those for only 17s.6d. He went on to say that it was unnecessary for him to comment upon the obvious inadequacy of such remuneration for offices of trust which cannot be satisfactorily filled but by persons of good education well trained in the habits of business.

Needless to say – as happens sometimes now – the postal system of the day led to communication problems. Thomas Parker, the Superintendent Registrar of Lewisham, was already writing to Thomas Lister in 1837 pointing out that, although the 3d. pacquet from London covered all Lewisham he had several times had to go or send to the General Post Office in London to collect parcels because they were over the 4oz. limit. Later, on the 3rd of March 1838, the certified for the December Quarter were duly sent off – the five Registrars having made a total of 74 Birth entries and 128 Death entries, while marriages in the Parish Churches totalled 58 entries. The copies did not arrive and were thought to be lost. Some heated correspondence took place between Thomas Parker and the Inspector of the Post Office. The packets were eventually discovered at the twopenny Post Office, being held back because they were overweight.

The 1836 Acts laid down that the Registration system was to be directed by the Registrar General, suitably staffed in London. Furthermore, it set out in broad outline the way in which the new service was to operate. No payment was to be required from the persons applying to have the event registered. Six weeks were allowed for the registration of a Birth. If registered after this time there would be a fee to be paid of 7s.6d. A Birth could not be registered at all after six months. This went on until 1874 when the responsibility of registering the Birth passed to the parents or the occupier of the place where the Birth took place, or to the persons in charge of the child. Five days was allowed for a Death registration. However, the actual 'policing' of this system was surely often inadequate – to the frustration of modern searchers after their ancestors – as many Births and Deaths seem to have escaped registration at all.

The Registrar General was required to provide a sufficient number of register books for making entries of all Births, Deaths and marriages in the precise form set out in the schedules appended to the Act. Each register contained spaces for five hundred entries and when a volume was completed it was to be returned to the local Superintendent Registrar.

Local Registrars were required to send copies of the entries in their registers in the preceding quarter to their Superintendent Registrar who, after verifying them, was to forward them to the Registrar General in London, so enabling a national Register to be established.

In his first annual report the Registrar General Thomas Lister describes the care he took to see that the procedure was properly and promptly carried out. He goes on to say how the copies were checked and queries followed up before they were sorted and bound into volumes. The final process was the preparation of a quarterly alphabetical index for England and Wales for Births, Deaths and Marriages separately. He reports that in the first year of registration, ending on the 30th of June 1838, these volumes contained no less than 958,630 entries. This was a considerable achievement. In the days when there were no typewriters, telephones, computers or emails it is all the more remarkable. Especially so when measured against the sneers of one of the speakers when the original Bill was discussed in the House of Lords in July 1836. That speaker suggested that the proposal was practically impossible inasmuch that the Registrar General would have to receive every year 88,000 separate papers, all of which he must classify. In addition, the Registration Act also set out rules for guaranteeing the safety of the registers. The Registrar was to supply a sufficient number of strong iron boxes to hold the register books. Every such box was to be furnished with a lock and two keys, one to be held by the Registrar General and one by the Superintendent Registrar.

When George Graham, who had been a Major in the East India Company, succeeded Thomas Lister as Registrar General in 1842 he inherited a system which was already well established. It needed developing and expanding. In certain areas a tightening-up and a rather more legal backing was required as he thought it was overstaffed and inefficient. Graham sacked the Chief Clerk and the Office Keeper, the latter for embezzlement. Very soon after he took office he wrote to the Home Secretary in December 1843 saying that he was concerned about the discreditable state of some of the Register Offices. Particularly about the lack of security, and that he had to dismiss four Registrars. He proposed that four inspectors should be appointed. The Treasury agreed that the appointments should be for one year only at a salary of £300 per annum. There would be an allowance for tavern expenses and four guineas a week for travelling expenses.

One of the problems was that by paying Registrars by entry there was a temptation for the unscrupulous and greedy to make fictitious entries. In the All Souls Sub-District of Marylebone between 1840 and 1844, for example, this was carried on to such a scale that it led to a recalculation of the district's Birth rate and the prosecution of the Registrar for felony. Elsewhere in the Great Howard Sub-District in Liverpool, the Registrar was prosecuted for a similar offence. The Magistrate had taken the view that it was a serious matter and as a felony it must go to trial. Mr. Chubb, for the defence, had requested bail. Mr. Snowball, for the prosecution, said he should have to oppose bail as it was a serious felony. There were a great many more such cases. "More cases, did you say?" said the Magistrate. "Yes," said Mr. Snowball. "I shall not then grant bail and the prisoner stands remanded until tomorrow." At the trial the defendant was found guilty by the jury and sentenced to six months imprisonment with hard labour.

There are many such incidents which the Street-wise enquirer may discover, and he or she should be alert to the complexities of Registration, and to some of its evident frustrations. There was never total accuracy at the time of each Census, and enumerators relied on people's own, or their neighbour's, accounts of their lives. Some parts of the UK were left off in several Censuses, notably including scattered islands, as Roger Hutchinson's analysis shows. In the early Census work not all parishes were included in the returns. Memory often failed people, too, and the truth was not always told – for example, concerning marital status. Bigamy, which was a crime, was not admitted to enumerators, and false names were given to conceal it on marriage certificates and in the Census. Not every mother was a married woman, and not every baby was baptised. Not every woman who earned a living from vice volunteered accurate data, and seeking to trace the origins and later years of such lives can indeed be hard.

Estimates of ages can be very misleading, too. The 1821 Census was the first to require a rough estimation by the enumerators of the ages of citizens, with enumerators asked to obtain estimated ages within a five or ten-year margin. However, this requirement was not included in the 1831 Census, although that did include employment information. Even when asked in later Censuses some people did not know their true birth date, or even where it had happened. Many tramps, beggars and others must have been missed altogether by the enumerators, too – accidentally or by the act of the individual concerned, particularly in the complex warrens, courtyards and alleys of over-crowded cities.

Chapter 3: UK Census Returns

The Street-wise enquirer will soon appreciate that the Census returns are not only important genealogically in general terms. They are also crucial because they will give you specific detailed access into a picture of the household of your family in the past. Where they were living, how old they were, what their marital status was, their occupations, their children. And – for tracing your family further back in time – they will (usually) provide that vital piece of information as to where they were born and when.

The term 'census' derives from the Latin word *censere*, which means to assess. The idea of taking a national Census was first thought of in 1756. And there was considerable opposition to this – with the same objections put forward as there were when a national identity card was proposed recently. In 1756 many of the Members of Parliament said that a Census would be an infringement of civil liberty and personal freedom. It was not until 1801, when the population was expanding rapidly, that the first national Census return was taken. It was an entirely new concept and an unprecedented work of government.

The Anglican cleric The Reverend Thomas Malthus had suggested that population growth would eventually outstrip the food production. In his book *An Essay on the Principle of Population,* first published in 1798 and regularly revised, Malthus said that an increase in a nation's food production certainly improved the well-being of the populace. But that the improvement was only temporary because it would lead to population growth, which would again reduce the standard of living. This idea became known as the "Malthusian trap". He wrote in opposition to the idea society was improving: "The power of population is indefinitely greater than the power in the earth to produce subsistence for man." Malthus urged that the increase of population is necessarily limited by the means of subsistence, that population does invariably increase when the means of subsistence increase, and that the superior power of population is repressed by moral restraint, vice and misery. This was an influential, if false idea.

Even when the Census was instituted – by the 'Act for taking an

Account of the Population of Great Britain' in 1801 – the early Censuses were very limited in the information that they gathered. And so the first four Censuses of 1801, 1811, 1821 and 1831 are of no use to family historians as they were merely a count of heads. In addition, most of the first four Census returns were also actually destroyed by government order in 1904, leaving us with only a few returns and some general reports. But from 1841 to 1911 the Censuses are a goldmine for England, Wales and Scotland. Alas, for Ireland (which did not formally become part of the United Kingdom until 1 January 1801) most of the nineteenth-century Censuses are not available, although Ireland was included in the 1821 Census for the first time.

There are some online fragments of the returns from 1821 through to 1851. But the full Irish Census papers taken between 1821 and 1851 were lost in the fire at the records office in Mason's 'Record Tower' in Dublin Castle in 1922 during the Irish Civil War, and the original Irish returns for 1861 and 1871 were thrown away shortly after being collated. Those for 1881 and 1891 were pulped during the Great War paper shortage. (Similarly, the 1931 Census for England and Wales was lost in a fire at its Middlesex storage warehouse in 1942). The 1901 and 1911 returns are available online at the National Archives of Ireland. There was no Census taken in Ireland in 1921 due to the convulsions there. From 1921 the UK Census covered only England, Scotland, Wales, and Northern Ireland. The 1926 Census was taken after the separation of Ireland in 1922. The first Census of the Irish Free State was taken on 18 April 1926. The first separate UK Census of the six northern counties was taken on that day too. As to the survival of Census data in Scotland we have not suffered any loss. But South Africa, after taking the data, shredded theirs, as did Australia. A good proportion of the Censuses for America and Canada are, however, available online.

The dates of the UK national Censuses were as follows: 6th June 1841, 30th March 1851, 7th April 1861, 2nd April 1871, 3rd April 1881, 5th April 1891, 31st March 1901, and 2nd of April 1911. All these returns have a catalogue number so you can access them. For 1841 and 1851 the catalogue number is HO 107, because at that time the Home Office was responsible for them. In 1861 the catalogue number changes to RG9 Registrar General. So RG10 is 1871, RG11 is 1881, RG12 is 1891, RG13 is 1901 and RG14 is 1911.

The Street-wise enquirer will be glad to know that the 1921 Census will in time be released. But the 1931 return was destroyed by fire and the 1941 return was not taken because of the war. There is a letter dated the 22nd of December 1942 from W. A. Derrick of the General Register Office to T. Stobart of the Central National Registration Office at Southport saying that last Saturday evening a fire gutted the Office of Works at Hayes which contained the 1931 Census returns and they were completely destroyed. The fire was not the result of enemy action. But that it spread so rapidly is a mystery, for the store had several hydrants fitted which were said to be under the charge of a fire guard of six paid watchers. The Census of 1931 had been the first to record people 'out of work'. The next Census was in April 1951.

Until the 1911 Census returns were released early there was the hundred year rule under which they were closed for a hundred years – so that for instance the 1881 return was not released until the 1st of January 1982. How soon the 1921 return will be available now that the commercial interest in early release is powerful we shall have to wait and see. As to the future, there is now talk that as so much of our data is already known it will not be necessary to take a Census in the future.

The following is an extract from Act 3 and Act 4 Victoria (the 3 and 4 referring to the year of her reign): "An Act for taking an Account of the Population of Great Britain. Penalty for refusing information or giving false answers. And the better to enable the said Commissioners, Enumerators, Schoolmasters and other Persons employed in the execution of this Act to make the said Inquiries and Returns be it enacted that they shall be authorised to ask all such questions as shall be directed in the Instructions to be issued by the said Commissioners.

"Every person refusing to answer or wilfully giving false answer to such questions or any of them shall for each such refusal or wilfully false answer forfeit a sum not more than £5 nor less than forty shillings at discretion of the Justice of the Peace or Magistrate before whom the complaint has been made.

"The above may be shown by the enumerator to any person refusing to answer or by questioning his authority to require an answer or giving an answer which he suspects to be false."

The 1841 return starts with the name of the parish at the top of the form and then it contains the place of residence of the people. In the larger cities you will probably not find a house number. The entry will just say Kingsland Road, Charles Street or Essex Place. Then it has the members of the household. The Street-wise enquirer should appreciate that the entry will only give an approximate age as this was rounded down. Thus, if a person was 22 they could be entered as 20.

But the exact age for children under 16 was supposed to be given. Thus, for Persons aged: 15 years and under 20, write 15. 20 years and under 25, write 20.
25 years and under 30, write 25. 30 years and under 35, write 30.
35 years and under 40, write 35. 40 years and under 45, write 40.
45 years and under 50, write 45. 50 years and under 55, write 50.
55 years and under 60, write 55. 60 years and under 65, write 60.
65 years and under 70, write 65. 70 years and under 75, write 70.
And so on, up to the greatest ages.

If no more can be ascertained respecting the age of any person that is a child or is grown up, you will only have "under 20" or "above 20" as the case may be. The occupation is usually only given for the head of the household. The next column is for the place of birth and here you will see "Yes" or "No" given. If the person lived in the county and were born in that county they answered "Yes". If they lived in the county but you were born elsewhere they (or the enumerator) put down "No". If they were born in Scotland the entry reads "S", "I" for Ireland, or "F" for foreign.

The 1841 Census was taken in pencil. And so sometimes the information remains hard to read. And errors in transcription must be considered, too. However, the content of the 1841 return can be very useful for those persons who lived to be over, say, 50, for this will take you back to the later decades of the eighteenth century.

You need to be aware of the occupational abbreviations used. Thus, F.S is for Female Servant, M.S for Male Servant, Ind for Independent, App for Apprentice, JY for a Journeyman – which could apply to several trades, the word originating from the French *jour* for day. The individual concerned will have served an apprenticeship and work by the day. Annuit is an Annuitant whose income is derived from an annuity.

In 1851 – although the general machinery and organisation for the taking of the Census returns remained unchanged – the scope of enquiry was greatly extended, the most important change being the giving of the parish where the individual was born, and their exact age (as given to the enumerator). But the Street-wise enquirer may entertain some suspicious uncertainty here; many did not know when they were, and sometimes even where they were born. We cannot be sure, either, who provided the information, or how well informed they were. If the enumerator did not interview the individual concerned, who made the report? Another family member? A neighbour? In 1851 coverage was widened to include all persons on board vessels in harbour or on navigable rivers. The Master of each vessel completed the schedule and then handed it to an Officer of the Customs who acted as an enumerator. In 1871 a request was made for the word "unemployed" to be added to the occupational description of persons engaged in some industry but out of employment.

Coming forward up to the 1881 return, the format remained the same. In the 1891 return there was a change, for this asked whether the individual inhabited four rooms or less. This question continued for the 1901 and 1911 returns. Sometimes you will find a family that has perhaps five or six children who only live in two rooms. Obviously there were always many cases of overcrowding. The 1911 return shows how long a couple have been married and how many children they have had, and how many are living and how many have died. This can be misleading, as if it is a remarriage – one or other having been widowed during the decade – no evidence is given as to previous marriages or on any issue from those marriages.

This I think can be misleading if the woman was a widow who had remarried between 1901 and 1911, and it only gives the number of children she has with her second or even third husband, for example.

The final column is a little bit intrusive one might say because it asks for information on whether the respondents were blind or deaf or dumb. They were later allowed to add whether a person was an idiot, a lunatic, or an imbecile and whether someone was a cripple or an invalid. You do find people registered as partially or blind from birth. I have found a woman who had three children and was blind from birth, and people who were given as deaf and also deaf and dumb. Some time ago there was a lady who was a consultant at Moorfields, the famous London eye hospital, who worked for a very long time in the Census returns for people identified in this way, for genetic research.

When you are researching Census returns it is most important that you examine all the available returns to follow your family through because people do have a tendency to give different information on different returns. Apart from actual ages they are quite good at changing the place where they were born even when it is in a close vicinity. You may find somebody will say Sussex and then say on one return Upmarden, next time East Marden. And, just to confuse matters further, North Marden. All three parishes will have Parish Registers so all three registers may have to be searched in order to establish the correct family.

You can also check out the ages to see whether they do tally – whether they are telling the truth or not. So some ladies seem to stay the same age from one decade to another. You can also follow the returns through to see if they had a change of occupation. The occupations are interesting. In Lancashire you get many people involved in the cotton trade; in Yorkshire it is in the woollen trade. Then in different parts of the country you get the local occupation. I have found Straw Hat Maker, Straw Plaiters, Buttonhook Makers, Glove Makers and Silk Weavers, for instance.

Another reason why it is important to follow the returns through is that new people do suddenly appear in the household. On one return you may find a couple with half a dozen children. On the next return a widowed father or mother or a father-in-law or mother-in-law will be living with the couple. With this knowledge it is possible to extend the family back another generation. Brothers and sisters up from the country can arrive in the family and if it is the mother's sister or brother born in the same area you will get the maiden name of the wife.

It seems to be a characteristic of the nineteenth century that there was a shortage of Christian names. You rarely find a person with two names and not often with an initial for the second name. You have to consider whether people with the same names given on successive Census returns are actually the same people. A William on, say, the 1851 return with a wife called Elizabeth and a William at the same address on the 1861 return may or may not be married to the same Elizabeth. The first Elizabeth may have died and William remarried during the decade. This may show up if there is a break in the birth of their children – for instance if you see a child of twelve and the next child is aged six.

One of the vital strategies when searching the returns is to think of every possible variant of the name you are researching. You also have to remember that when the return was filled in some people were barely literate and the Enumerator would try to help. But with the strong regional accents misunderstandings must have taken place. Then there is the great difficulty with the capital letter of the surname, as many can look confusingly similar when written by hand. H and K, B and R spring to mind, not to mention S and L. Also consider that sometimes people are just put down as initials such as P D or M H. This usually happens in institutions such as Workhouses, Lunatic Asylums or Hospitals.

A little about local Censuses, which were first begun as early as 1522 and continued until 1930: they are in no way connected to the national Census. They are useful in population growth and population movement. What can be considered as a Census are Poll Books, Hearth Tax, Window Tax and Protestation Oaths. There are also Easter Books, if they survive. These usually record all full members of the Church of England, the Communicant Lists and Examinations. These latter items exist for Scotland. In addition for Scotland there are the Examination of Catechismal Inhabitants Lists. These were Lists for those who had been examined for their knowledge of the catechism. The Lists were compiled usually by the Church of Scotland ministers. It is not clear how early people were examined but it has been suggested that this was from the age of eight upwards. The examinations were repeated annually and if they survive they are a good source for people of all ages.

Between 1801 and 1811 there are well over 750 small individual Censuses which were taken. Generally they listed only the head of the household and they say, for example, "four males and two females".

The 1939 Register was taken at the outbreak of the Second World War. Details of about forty million people were taken in England and Wales. The National Registration was on the 29th of September that year. It is available online at Find my Past. It was also taken in Scotland and Northern Ireland but they are not online. They can, however, be applied for at the relevant Office.

Sometimes you find an address on a certificate, say the 29th of March, and the return is taken on the 3rd of April but yet the individuals have moved on. In the big cities people who lived in two or three rooms did not have much furniture. They might only have a couple of orange boxes, a bed with a table and some pots and pans, so it was on to a barrow and move to a few streets away. This often happened if they could not pay the rent, and was known as "a moonlight flit". However, if people depended on credit at local shops where they were known, on help from other family members or from neighbours, and on possible employment locally they often did not move very far. So check nearby streets too. You need to be aware that abbreviations and even some curious wrong words were used by enumerators. For example, the abbreviation "Middx" has been found to be given as "Mexico", and "Cockes Jockes" turned out to be Cockfosters, in Hertfordshire.

I still find it quite amazing that when I first started looking at Census returns, the 1871 was not available, the returns then being closed for a hundred years. You still saw the original documents for the Censuses then as they were open to see. They used to come up in a cardboard box, you lifted the lid and there was the return. Later on they were microfilmed and you spent much time turning the handle. And the family you wanted were often on folio 404, after which you had to turn the film all the way back. Considering everything, the survival rate of our national records is really exceptionally good. There have been important acts of rescue and recovery too. In Manchester in 1851 water got in and they were quite badly damaged, but the Manchester Family History Society has done excellent work and have managed to bring up the images. Another loss was of Pimlico in London in 1861.

Lastly, the Street-wise enquirer will always be alert to problems created by the inputting of information into digital form. Those concerned have done their utmost, and much has been done by volunteers. But there are still some inaccuracies online. So check alternative sources. For example, if you cannot find it on Ancestry then try Find my Past. FreeCen has begun putting the returns online. This is an easy to use site and is free.

A recent useful discussion is Roger Hutchinson, *The Butcher The Baker The Candlestick Maker. The Story of Britain Through its Census, since 1801* (London, Little Brown, 2017), which is full of out of the way research information and thoughtful reflections.

Chapter 4: From the Parish Register

These are an essential source for all Street-wise enquirers. Together with Civil Registration and the Census returns, they are the most valuable sources of genealogical information available to family historians. We are indeed fortunate that so many do survive. They can provide information which can be found nowhere else. Many have survived to tell us the stories of the important events in the lives of our ancestors – namely the baptisms, marriages and burials. They also sometimes give an indication of the harshness of those former times from notes in the margins of the registers.

This is a summary of the most important dates in the history of the development of Parish Registers. I also advise that they as a source should never be used in isolation. The Parish Chest material can contain within the Overseers Accounts, the Highway Accounts and other documents such a wealth of data as to how our ancestors lived.

From 1538 every Anglican parson, vicar or curate was to enter in a book every wedding, christening and burial which took place in his parish with the names of the parties. They were to be kept safely in a coffer with two locks. A coffer was a chest in which valuables could be kept. The parson would have one key and the Churchwardens the other. The entries for the preceding week were to be entered each Sunday in the presence of the incumbent and one of the Churchwardens. These entries were generally made in paper books or even at times on loose or odd sheets, and it was not until 1598 that there was a change in this procedure. As so often happens, any new law is met with suspicion, and with anxiety that changes would lead to the imposition of a tax.

In 1598 the Provincial Constitution of Canterbury required that the registers should be made of parchment books and that all previous entries from 1538 onwards would be transferred to these books, particularly those since the accession of Queen Elizabeth in 1558. This latter statement was in many cases taken advantage of as an excuse not to copy entries prior to 1558, and so many of the earlier registers have been lost to us. It was also ordered that two Churchwardens should witness the entries. Finally, the Churchwardens should within a month of Easter submit a transcript of the registers to the Diocesan Registry for the preceding year. These became known as Bishops' Transcripts. I will return to them a little later.

In September 1538, following the Reformation and after the suppression of the Pilgrimage of Grace and the Lincolnshire Uprising, Parish Registers were commenced. The period covered by the Civil War and the Commonwealth 1642–1660 was a desperate time for the keeping of Parish Registers. Many clergy – especially if they had Royalist sympathies – were ejected from their living. And the Barebones Parliament in 1653 passed an Act which deprived ministers of their keeping of the registers and also forbade the solemnisation of marriages. Of course, viewed in the context of over four hundred and fifty years of Parish Registers, this eighteen years was a comparatively short space of time and the effects were haphazard, with some incumbents keeping no records at all. There were registers that were buried for safety, some were destroyed and others in the general turmoil lost forever. And yet again others appear to have been kept as usual.

At the Restoration of the Monarchy in 1660 the clergy who had survived returned to the parishes and gradually things returned to normal. Many children had been left unbaptised and the Ministration of Baptism to people such as were of riper years was approved by the Convocation of 1661. A number of adult baptisms begin at this time to appear in the register, so all enquirers who have lost baptisms around this period, do not give up hope.

During the years that followed, various Acts were passed, including the Burial in Woollen in 1666 in an effort to encourage the wool trade, but this gradually petered out and was eventually repealed in 1814. An Act of 1680 by which parents were ordered to register each birth for a fee of 6d. was largely ignored and in 1694 a tax on Birth, Marriage and Burial on a sliding scale was introduced, ranging from £30 for the birth of the eldest son of a Duke down to 2s. for lesser mortals. A Duke's marriage and burial were £50 each, relating to 2s.6d and 4s. at the other end of the scale. Births were to be notified to the incumbent within five days and he was to receive a fee of 6d. for recording them. It was especially provided that a birth should not be exempt from tax because the parents failed to have the child baptised. There was a penalty of 40s. for failing to notify a birth within five days.

As always, some parishes were more law-abiding than others but the tax was short-lived, as evidenced by the fact that an Act of Indemnity was passed on behalf of the clergy in 1705 who had neglected to obey the Act.

In the year 1678 there was an Act of Parliament which was again intended to encourage the manufacture of woollen cloth. It laid down that nobody should be "put in, wrapt up or wound up, or buried in any shirt, shift, sheet, or shroud made or mingled with flax, hemp, silk, hair, gold, or silver or other than what is made of sheep's wool only". The relatives of the deceased were required to bring to the Minister, within eight days of the burial, an affidavit certifying that the requirements of the law had been fulfilled. The penalty for non-compliance was £5, half of which went to the informer and half to the poor of the Parish. Sadly, none have survived.

Early registers up to the early 1700s were often written in Latin but you will find that a simple Latin Glossary will help you with the most used words. You will, however, encounter some difficult handwriting, for some vicars wrote appallingly. I well remember when we were compiling our Sussex Burial Index one vicar who had been in his parish for a very long time – some 50 years or so – and his writing got worse and worse until at last just after his last entry was his own burial entry.

In the seventeenth century you will often find a duplication of the same Christian name in the baptismal register. You will see James son of Samuel and Ann, and two years later the entry repeated and again later the same entry. There are two possible reasons for this. In the time of very high infant mortality, with a desire to see the name continued in the family, the first or even the second child may have died or the first child may be very sickly with the possibility of early death. So it was considered important to make sure that the name was established. At this time Godparents played an important role in a child's upbringing and it would also be appropriate and perhaps farsighted to name the child with the name of the Godparent. There was only a limited choice of Christian names and so it would be quite possible to choose a Godparent with the same Christian name as the child.

Many of the seventeenth- and eighteenth-century registers were entered at a later date from possibly a memorandum book or a rough notebook kept for the purpose of recording the events. And so it often happens that this is when mistakes can occur. Sometimes it has been suggested that the clerk would not even do this and only kept very haphazard notes to be used as an *aide memoir* such as "Thomas Brown's child buried" or "Thomas Brown's wife buried". When the register came to be written, perhaps when it was time to make the copies for the Bishops' Transcripts to be returned, there was a panic and nobody could actually remember the name of Thomas Brown or John son of John Brown or John son of John Brown and his wife. Most frustrating. This custom of keeping the rough notes was specifically forbidden by Rose's Act of 1812. From 1813 corrections are sometimes found in the margin of the register – for example, saying that this child was entered as William but it should be John and the vicar signs the alteration.

The most important Act for Family Historians was that of Lord Hardwick's Marriage Act of 1753, which came into force in 1754. The Act was actually called an Act for the Better Preventing of Clandestine Marriages. This title always to me conjures up pictures of heiresses climbing out of the castle to elope with the waiting groom and living happily ever afterwards. The main thrust of the Act though was against what were legal marriages despite having been performed by a priest without licence or banns. Hardwick's Act declared that a marriage could only take place after the publication of banns or by a licence issued by a Bishop of the diocese. Banns and Marriage registers were to be kept separate from registers of baptisms and burials for the first time. The information on the printed entry form was fairly basic, typically: "John Smith of Balcombe bachelor and Ann Howard of this parish spinster 4th May 1755. Witnesses Thomas Howard, Benjamin Cross by banns." The bride and groom, the witnesses and the officiating minister signed the register.

Sometimes both parties were given as 'of this parish' and their marital status could be given as bachelor, spinster, widow or widower. Mostly the marriage took place in the bride's parish. The marriage could take place by licence or by banns. The latter were required to be called for three succeeding weeks before the marriage could take place in the parishes of both the bride and the groom. The only exceptions to the Act were Quakers and Jews who it was considered kept such satisfactory records that it was not necessary for them to comply with the Act.

Licences, meanwhile, were issued by church authorities and enabled people to be married quickly without waiting for the banns to be read. The more well-to-do availed themselves of this, as did those in need of a hasty marriage, and sometimes soldiers and sailors who might be called away at short notice.

The records of a marriage licence – if they are still extant – are known as the Allegation. This was a declaration on oath by the bride and groom of their freedom to marry. The Bond was a record of security given usually by a relation or close friend to the truth of this, and the Licence a document authorising marriage which could often be at a stipulated church. The distinct disadvantage of the format of the entry under Lord Hardwick's Act is that the names of the fathers are not given for either party, and so it does not help at all in establishing a further generation. Nor is the occupation of the bride or groom given. Very often, again, the second witness is a Churchwarden and you will see his name occurs frequently in the register. This format continued up to 1st July 1837 when Civil Registration began.

The next landmark is known as Rose's Act, 1812, drafted by Sir George Rose and implemented in 1813. It was passed for the better regulating and preserving of parish and other registers for baptisms, marriages and burials, but the marriage format remained the same. From now on baptisms and burials would be kept in separate registers. The format consisted of columns in the case of baptisms. For example, I have copies dated 12th July 1814 giving George, son of John and Ann Howard, Balcombe, aged 64. In a small parish you find only the name of the parish is given as an address, but in larger towns you may sometimes get the street and sometimes in a village you will get a hamlet or the name of a farm. As you will see, the information at this time is still sparse and it is most frustrating that the maiden name of the mother is not given. In the burial register you will have the date of burial, the name of the person buried, the abode and the age. This is a very important addition as prior to 1813 it was not required by law to give the age at burial. So you can only guess whether the entry was for a 20, 30, 40, 50 year old, or older person. You may find John Harris given only as the infant son of Henry and Sarah Taylor.

We are also still at the whim of the parish incumbent. Some did enter in the burial register a cause of death, especially so if there was a smallpox outbreak, for instance. Others may have added the marital status or in the case of children the name of the father and mother. In the baptismal register illegitimate children are recorded as baseborn or bastard child. I remember one vicar in the 1820s who in the baptism register gave the occupation, peasant, to the father of the child to many of his flock. A burial register at about the same time in a large town sometimes gave the name of the doctor who attended the deceased along with the cause of death.

The format for baptisms and burials continued after the commencement of Civil Registration on the 1st of July 1837. Entries are most useful for the first twenty years or so of this period since many births were not registered during this time and so at least we have a baptismal record to help us in our searches. You will notice in the baptismal registers the wording "privately baptised". This could happen if the baby was ill or likely to die before it could be brought to church for baptism and received into the church. Another entry you may see is that of a woman being churched after a birth. That is because it was in Leviticus that a woman was unclean after giving birth so she needed to be readmitted into the church.

I would like now to return briefly to the Bishops' Transcripts. As mentioned earlier, these were started in 1598. Their survival rate is mixed and some are more complete than others. Sometimes, as in Sussex, there are about 40 parishes where they pre-date the Parish Registers which have been lost or destroyed and so those obviously are most useful. The quality of transcripts varies enormously, some having been written on scraps of paper a few inches square and others on large sheets written sometimes in a very higgledy-piggledy way. The transcripts were not highly thought of at the Bishop's Registries, and as numbers grew over the years they were often bundled up and put in out-of-the-way places and when eventually found were in very poor condition. Despite this, they do at times contain differences from the Parish Registers, and omissions should if possible be checked against each other – especially if an entry, you feel, should be in the register but is not found.

The amount of detail found in the Registers at all times is dependent on the incumbent. For instance, five children of the same family may all have been buried within four weeks of each other, but there is nothing added to satisfy our curiosity as to what occurred. Whereas, by contrast, an entry in the burial register of the little parish of Rolliston in Derbyshire tells us about the family whose name was Lovely; that they were newcomers to the parish; and, between 24th of May and the 30th July 1877, first Henry aged 4 was buried, followed by Samuel 17, John aged 10, then Sarah Ann 13, the baby Charles 10 months and finally Emma aged 3. There is no reference to any other family suffering so and no evidence of an epidemic in the village. How did parents survive having so many of their family literally wiped out in such a short space of time?

On 7th of January 1834 William Goodsell aged 22 of Ewhurst was buried, and the entry noted that he was hanged for arson at Horsham. There is a newspaper account of the hanging which took place on the 4th of January. During his time in prison awaiting trial he told the chaplain that he attributed his fall to drinking, gaming and frequenting beer houses. His crime was that he had set fire to a barn. A thousand people, including many women and children, watched the hanging, after which he was cut down and his friends put him in a coffin and took him back to Ewhurst.

The Street-wise enquirer should also be aware of some other important points. Firstly, prior to 1813, no age at burial is given in burial registers and no occupation. It was not required by law – but as always in genealogy there is ever the exception and if you get what I would call a chatty vicar he may well give the age, and that you can consider a bonus in your research. Also, prior to 1813, no occupation is given in the baptismal registers and no maiden name of the mother. You will also always find variations of spelling – 'e' and 's' dropped off or added to the end of a name, aitches lost and 'a' and 'o' which look remarkably alike. If I said to you my name is Cook, for instance, you would have no idea whether there was an 'e' on the end or not. Such names as Anna and Hannah were sometimes put down wrongly. Many immigrant names were changed and Anglicised, also.

Some Puritan names may have been used, too: Repentance, Praise God, Safe on High and Dust and Ashes, Sin Denie and Deliverance.

The Old Style Calendar can be confusing. Up until 1752 the beginning of the Year was on 25th March – Lady Day. In 1751 the Gregorian or New Style Calendar was adopted by Act of

Parliament. The first day after the 31st December became the 1st of January 1752 (this would previously have been 1st of January 1751 or 1st January 1751/52). To assist in the change examples were set by King George III (who had been born on the 24th May 1738), who changed his birthday to the 4th June and by John Wesley, the famous Non-Conformist preacher, who changed his from 17th June to 28th June.

Then there are the important Non-Conformist registers. Practically all of these were deposited at the Public Record Office, now the National Archives at Kew. They were centralised in 1840 and in some ways this was very helpful in the conservation and we could wish that more care had been taken similarly of our own Parish Registers. Many Non-Conformist registers are available online, and on Family Search (the free site of the Jesus Christ Church of the Latter Saints).

Of course, it must always be remembered that fire, flood, damp and war damage and mice have all played their part in depriving us of many Parish Registers over the centuries. Not forgetting the human hand. I am thinking of a vicar's wife who actually made lampshades from the parchment and the other good lady who decided to make kettle holders for Christmas gifts for the needy poor. Also, when an actual entry was needed as proof in a peerage claim, several pages were cut out of the register to establish the claim. Despite this, Parish Registers are sometimes the only record of our ancestors because, of course, we are not all lucky enough to be related to members of the professions, soldiers or sailors, who leave behind records of their physical descriptions, or the criminals, the tradesmen, the heroes, the teachers, and the politicians who leave behind many other sources which we can use in pursuit of fleshing out the bare bones. For me, like many others, we have only those who are hatched, matched and despatched.

It is to be regretted that church registers instituted by Royal injunction in 1538 were but little cared for during the last century. For example, those at Rivington in Lancashire which tradition relates were destroyed by fire. When I started family history the first question was where were the Parish Registers which had to be consulted, and how did you locate them, especially when some of the incumbents you asked were none too sure of their whereabouts. The passing of the Parochial Registers and Records Measure in 1978 (which became law on the 1st of January 1979) was a great achievement. The background to this is I think of interest. In 1976, concerned in general about the safe keeping and conservation of Parish Registers and records, my husband introduced a bill in the House of Lords known as the Parish Registers and Records Bill. On second reading a Bishop – he now cannot remember which one but he thinks it was the Bishop of London – said that the General Synod of the Church of England would take on this legislation and pass a Measure which would protect the records. The results of their deliberations were then presented to the Joint Parliamentary Ecclesiastical Committee which consisted of members of both Houses (my husband was a member of this Committee) for their approval. There were one or two points which were considered not to be approved, so the measure was sent back to the Synod. It was then returned to the Committee with a hint that if it were not approved this time it would be dropped. Fortunately for us it was approved. After this it had to be approved on the floor of both Houses. This was successful and it was passed in 1978.

The County Records Offices are the places to start your work. The situation varies county by county. At first, for Parish Register entries, we had the Computer File Index produced by The Church of Jesus Christ of Latter-day Saints followed by the International Genealogical Index (first issued in 1973) and which now contains several million entries. Both were a great help in locating entries, although some counties have limited records. Because of opposition from the local Bishop, many were poorly covered by these ventures and only printed sources were allowed to be microfilmed. Cheshire, Essex and Northampton come to mind. Then in Sussex the situation was unsatisfactory because the Bishop in West Sussex was cooperative but the Bishop in East Sussex was not. In Durham and Northumberland – for a period from 1797 to 1812 – the Bishop of Northumberland and Durham kept what are known as the Bishop Shute Barrington Registers. The Bishop considered that entries should contain more details of the event than only those that were required by law. Even if the entry you are looking for is not in that period, it is quite possible that you could pick up a brother or sister, which would assist you in your searches.

Find My Past and Ancestry have many registers now on their sites. Parish Clerks can be useful too – searches can be done by county and are free. Family Search has already been mentioned.

This covers UK Parish Registers, UK Genealogy Archives covering Devon and Cornwall and some Derbyshire entries (and is also free). It is always worthwhile googling a parish or a county to see what has been transcribed and put on line.

In my own work I have found some odd entries over the years. Burial registers generally give the best value in odd entries. In 1606 William Beeny the son of Simon was buried on 29th December in a field adjoining to the house that his father dwelleth in because it was suspected that he had died of the plague. I think this was true, as the following January his brother Gyles was buried in the same manner, followed in February by his brothers Robert and Zabulon.

There are often people being buried when it is stated that they were a hundred years old. A very detailed entry is that for George Howell who was born 6th June 1754 at West Hoathly and died at Ditchling 7th May 1855 aged 100 years and 336 days. And there was a small engraving of this gentleman portraying him just after his hundredth birthday, dressed in a plain smock frock seated in a high-backed chair. The entry says that he was a Shoemaker of Ditchling. Similarly, Elizabeth Newman was buried on the 20th of November 1829 aged 100 and Frances Smith outdid her by being buried on the 10th of July 1837 aged 101.

At Salehurst in 1808 poor William Sinden aged 39 was buried after having been blown into five parts – his head, leg and thigh, body and one leg and thigh and arm – from the sudden explosion of Brede Gunpowder Mills.

Many children were burnt and scalded to death. There was a baby buried in 1834 aged two days who had been born in Horsham Jail. A touching entry for Charles Robert Bassett, buried on 5th February 1837, tells us of A Good Boy aged 7. For James Easemore it was noted when he was buried in 1825 by a Coroner's Inquest that he was a travelling pauper. One awful entry is when a farmer's wife, just after having a baby, took rat poison accidentally and took three days to die.

For marriages: in Seaford on the 15th of June 1749 William Taylor to his fourth wife Mary Vine and she to her fourth husband. I wonder how many children they had between them. The banns of marriage were published between Dovey Spencer and Mary

Hastings on the first Sunday but by the second Sunday he being a soldier had marched from the town. I should have searched the baptism register to see if a few months later a little Hastings had been baptised.

I have mentioned marriages by Licence and this is the type of entry you find – William Carter of Meeching otherwise Newhaven, Labourer Bachelor 19 and upwards with consent of Sarah Carter widow, his mother. Also, Dorothy Taylor of Beddingham spinster aged 19 and upwards with consent of Thomas Taylor her father bondsmen said WC and Wm Davies Beddingham, gent 21 May 1813. This was a very detailed entry and in this case for a fairly ordinary couple as he was only a labourer by occupation.

Then there was the burial of Mildred Reed Alfriston aged 24. Rumours having gone abroad that this young woman was buried alive, her grave was opened eleven days after her interment in the presence of the Minister of the Church and one of the Churchwardens. The medical gentleman who attended her in her last illness and a great multitude of people were there, and after an inspection of the body, there were perfectly satisfied that the rumour was unfounded, although an old man who is very deaf said he heard a noise proceed from the grave only two or three days before she was exhumed. Finally: in 1837 John Wakeford aged 24 killed in a pugilistic combat at Rogate. In Broadwater William Caplin aged 46 apoplexy died while about to drink a Horn of Beer. Verdict: excessive draught of beer.

Chapter 5: The Parish Chest

This evokes in the mind's eye an ancient wooden chest bound by hoops of iron and guarded by large locks and containing musty registers and note books with documents all written in a clear clerical hand which hold all the answers to all our questions about our ancestors.

Parish chests existed long before Parish Registers came into force in September 1538 and in those earlier days the medieval Churchwardens kept their accounts together with inventories of the church furnishings and utensils used in the services.

My period of the Parish Chest is basically between 1601, which saw the introduction of the Elizabethan Poor Law, and 1834 when the New Poor Law Act came into force and much of the responsibility of the parish was then passed to the civil authorities.

Like so many things, the 1601 Act was intended to be a temporary measure but it was prolonged in 1603/4 and made permanent in 1640 and thereafter stayed in force until 1834.

The Parish Chest contains documents that belong to the incumbent and the vestry. Records are not public as long as they relate entirely to ecclesiastical matters. The incumbent is assisted by two or more Churchwardens, dependent on the size of the parish. The Churchwardens are responsible for the upkeep of church property and the provision of the utensils for the service. The parish clerk is supposed to deal with the parish records, but he did not always carry out his duties as well as could be desired. The Reverend Caleb Collins ministered in Stedham and Heyshott from 1826 to 1879 – was it him or was it the clerk (one Henry Pope who was parish clerk there for many of those years) who kept all the Parish Register entries on scraps of paper so that the actual registers are bare of entries? There is a note that the incoming vicar found the baptisms for 1826 to 1839 on separate scraps of paper but those from 1840 to 1879 were still missing. This was in 1897 and it was some years later that these were eventually found, by which time it was impossible to say which entries were for Stedham and which for Heyshott. A fair old muddle all round.

The vestry or parish council was made up of reliable men

who were considered capable of seeing to the running and the organising of the parish. The vestry meeting was usually presided over or chaired by the incumbent and they worked in conjunction with the Justices of the Peace. There were two kinds of vestry meetings: closed, or sometimes called select, and open. Closed was the governing body of the parish and members usually had a property qualification, and open was a general meeting held periodically for all inhabitants of rate-paying households. So it will be seen that the Vestry Minutes can hold much genealogical information as to what happened in a parish. There are also the Parish Constables' Accounts and the two Surveyors of the Highway records. Also, the Glebe Terriers and the Tithe Records. And, probably most usefully, the Settlement papers in two parts (examination and removal certificates), Vagrancy, Bastardy and Apprentice records are included. I would like to take each in turn and give you examples of what can be found and I should say that many of these records are now deposited in the County Record Offices.

Churchwardens' Accounts

Mostly these are entries to do with the maintaining of the church fabric or additions to the church or rebuilding work. But you will find names such as John Verrall being paid one shilling for the killing of hedgehogs and other vermin, John Bushnell is mentioned for mending the prayer books, Henry Collins for buying the bread for Communion and William Sturgeon for cleansing the bells. Thomas Luck was paid seven shillings and sixpence for looking after the boys and keeping dogs out of the church. To prevent any breach of discipline or intrusion during divine service an official known as a Dog Whipper was paid an annual wage to keep watch and take preventive action if necessary. I wonder how often they got bitten.

Thomas Hosman was paid 30 shillings for looking after the clock and the chimes and for ringing the eight o'clock bell, this was in 1725, and in 1730 he was paid £12-10 shillings for shingling the steeple and in addition the clerk supplied him with beer. It was obviously very thirsty work. George Piper submits a bill for carrying nine loads of timber to the church from Cronesden for a fee of £2-5-0. This is of interest as Cronesden is not a parish but a farm or a hamlet perhaps within the parish and may give a clue as to where George Piper actually lived. Later in the accounts we come across entries for shingling the steeple and it must have eventually been in a very bad way because in 1791 there are very exact accounts for the work which was done, seventeen items noted in the bill which includes ten names. Also in the accounts are charities and in 1782 when Thomas Baker Esquire died he left a house and land to the vicar and Churchwardens in order that "weekly and every week forever loaves of good and wheaten flour should be given to the poor of the parish". There was a catch to the bequest, though, as the bread was to be given out on Sundays after the close of the afternoon service.

An entry to increase comfort in church is: "Whereas the first set on ye south side commonly called the churching seat was made more warm and convenient for that use by the Churchwardens in December 1727. We thereby acknowledge that the right of claim which Thakeham Place has unto the said seat is in no way injured thereby but to remain as before for the servants of Thakeham Place 9th March 1726/7 3."

Overseers Accounts

These accounts are of a much more personal nature and show how the poor were maintained and the sick and the aged were relieved. The Overseer was also responsible for the collection of the rate and this was of course vital importance, otherwise he would have no funds with which to administer his outgoings. He also apprenticed pauper children and made every attempt to stop anyone settling in the parish who might become a burden on the finances of the parish. I will go more thoroughly into the system of Settlement and Removal later on.

Items show up in the accounts such as: Paid to Widow Woods for 20 weeks from the 1st of December 1662 to the 20th April 1663, 4 shillings a week. Faggots for Widow Baker, (what an irritating habit of saying Widow so and so not giving us the Christian name!), two print dresses for Sarah Verrall to go into service with. John Freeman seems to have been well kitted out in 1728 as he was given a pair of breeches, a cap, stockings, a shirt and worsted. Samuel Stafford is perhaps even more fortunate as he is given leather to make him a coat, money for the thread and buttons and the Overseers paid for the making of the coat, and finally Mary Denyer was paid for the washing of his clothes. Illness shows up, 15 and 6 pence for Mary Frensham's bleeding and Master Pain was paid one shilling for curing Hester Higgins of the itch.

Another Widow, this time Widow Glover, cost the parish ten shillings for her coffin and the ringing of the bell plus two pounds for the wool to cover her, plus two pounds to heal Sarah Cooper's shoulder. John Eccles is given relief in his sickness and Charles Burrows paid for keeping Thomas Hunter, who presumably could have been a fostered-out orphan or perhaps an old man.

For transporting Francis Poulton from Mr. Garnet's barn to Weston beyond Bulldock, "being so rotten with smallpox as to not be able to walk or ride." "To widow Bigg of Wood Street, for nursing and taking care of Mary Green, found perished in the forest." (They gave her 5 shillings, and threepence for looking after Mary Green but the care wasn't sufficient because they also had to give the widow Bigg 7 shillings and nine pence for her funeral.) "To five naked Turkish galley slaves on their way home." (What would five naked Turkish galley slaves be doing walking through the English countryside? There is no explanation.) "To Mr. Bleen, the surgeon, for setting old Phoebe's arm." And then the next entry is "Laying out old Phoebe and her bearers for her coffin." "To widow Duck for being lame, and to Mr. Garnet for a horse and cart to carry widow Duck to the hospital."

The doctors' bills can be found also: Dr. Heasman charged for treating Thomas Smileman two shillings for letting blood to his head, one shilling for plasters to his stummick, one shilling for strong spirits, five shillings and sixpence for an electuary for his inward feaver and two shillings for mixtures. There is no record to say whether or not he survived the treatments. But we get names and more names as well as fascinating glimpses of how our ancestors lived.

Rate Books
From the mid-eighteenth century onwards – if they survive and if there is a good run – these are most helpful in research as they will give you the owner of the house but not always the name of the house. They will also give you the name of the tenant paying their rates.

Apprentices Records
There are some that have good lists and sometimes they are quite early, such as: 3rd of March 1634 Richard Tullie aged 10 bound apprentice to Thomas Loughton Gentleman also on the same day Elizabeth Turner bound apprentice to Ralph Poore Yeoman; 19th

May 1655, a time during the Commonwealth when records are scarce: Thomas Hards bound apprentice to Thomas Wilson of Buxted Miller, here we have the additional bonus of a place name and an occupation and on 7th April 1646 Joane Waghorn to John Stevenson, Carrier and his wife Ellen.

Apprentices are bound not to frequent taverns, inns or alehouses, not to play cards, dice or any other unlawful game. A rather dreary life you may feel, and one remembers the old saying, 'All work and no play makes Jack a dull boy'.

Sometimes you may find a paper on the boarding out of a pauper, for example: 23 Jan 1661 William and Joan Briggman husbandman agree to take the bastard child of Dorothy Christmas until the age of 14. Unfortunately, there is nothing to indicate the sex of the child but a look at the Parish Register might establish the event and so find whether it is a boy or a girl.

An example of Christmas Day in 1746. On 15 Oct 1746 Susan Browning of Henfield said that last summer she was placed out by Henfield Parish as an apprentice to Thomas Bennett of Fletching by indenture. She stayed with her master one month and then he sent her to her father who at that time lived at St Johns Common for a pair of shoes and that she stayed there two days and then returned to her master Thomas Bennett. She stayed there one more month and then her master beating her she went away again for a quarter of the year. But she returned before Christmas Day on which day she remembers they had for dinner a shoulder of mutton, plum pudding, white cabbage and turnips. She stayed with her master although he did beat her but she eventually ran away and she has ever since worked in various places.

Highway Accounts
They are concerned with the upkeep of the roads and give us more names – Henry Richardson for carrying fourteen loads of potsherds, William Reeves for 24 days of digging gravel and John Baker for the spreading of cinders, for instance.

Glebe Terriers
This is a term specific to the Church of England. Glebe Terriers were documents – usually a written survey or inventory – giving details of glebe, lands and property in the parish owned

by the Church of England and held by a clergyman as part of the endowment of his benefice. This provided the means by which the incumbent (the rector, vicar or perpetual curate) could support himself and his church. Typically, a glebe would comprise the vicarage or rectory, fields and the church building itself, its contents and its graveyard. If there was an absentee rector the glebe would usually be divided into a rectorial glebe and the rest. The word "Terrier" is derived from the Latin *terra*, "earth".

The glebe terrier would be drawn up at the time of each visitation, an official visit usually by the Archdeacon who would make an annual visit. The Bishop would also visitd outlying parts of his diocese every few years to maintain ecclesiastical authority and conduct Confirmations.

Each church was entitled to a house and glebe, with the glebe lands either being cultivated by the clergyman himself, or by tenants to whom he leased the land. There were parishes where the parsonage was not well-endowed with glebe, and in these cases the clergyman's main source of income would come from the tithes.

The Street-wise researcher should appreciate that Glebe terriers are useful historical documents as they may contain the names of tenants and the holders of adjoining lands. The Terrier can provide useful information on the strips and furlongs in the parish and may also contain information on how income from tithes was calculated and collected.

The information, where it survives, goes back a long way. The first full lists of the holdings of each parish were required in 1571. Inevitably, they vary greatly as the compilation of the survey was undertaken by and at the discretion of each individual clergyman. The surveys were then collected together in the Church of England Registries, but a copy was often kept in the parish. Many are now kept in county record offices.

Tithe Records

The introduction of the Tithe Commutation Act of 1836 meant records were taken, as with the Domesday Book, of the land ownership and occupancy, land use and sizes, and the rents to be paid. This affected all levels of the social hierarchy.

This is a potentially very fruitful area of personal documentation. We are fortunate that the National Archives website has a detailed guide to these pre-census records, and the Kew guide which is the best place to start. This explains what types of records were created as part of the Tithe Survey and how to search for them. It also refers to other records related to tithes. This guide helps you to find an ancestor who once lived in a given parish. It also offers information about a particular property. The Tithe Records provide a unique view of ownership and occupancy of land throughout England and Wales.

The records of the Tithe Survey may show where people were living and who their neighbours were. There is also material on crop acreages, field names, house occupancy, rights of way and parish boundaries. County Record Offices also hold such records.

'The National Collection of Tithe Records' has been provided by *The Genealogist* where you can search the records of over 11,000,000 parishes and view the original documents online. Maps with microfilm references are also shown.

Settlement Examinations and Removal Orders

These are an important source. In 1662 an Act known as the Act of Settlement was passed. Among other things it stated that a stranger staying in the parish could be removed by the Overseers within forty days if he had no means of being able to work or if he did not rent property worth £10 a year. After forty days a stranger could claim that he was settled in the parish and therefore if he was out of work, became ill or had an accident he could claim settlement, and so become a charge on the poor rate. This Act also entitled the Justices to punish persistent vagrants. Thirty-five years later in 1697 another Act of Settlement was passed and this stated that strangers were allowed to enter a parish provided that they possessed a settlement certificate showing that they would be taken back by their own parish if they needed to claim poor relief. The administration of the law often caused confusion, although the law itself is quite clear. I would point out that the parish of settlement was not always necessarily the parish of birth. A person was able to gain settlement in a parish:

By being born there if illegitimate.

By working there for at least a year if unmarried.

By working a full apprenticeship in the parish.
By a woman marrying her husband there.
By having a father there if the child was legitimate and under seven years of age.
By holding public office.
By paying rates or having forty days' residence thereafter giving due notice in writing.

This system led to what was known as the Examination by a magistrate and sometimes a formal interview to establish the person's parish, often very tricky because of lack of knowledge, sometimes genuine, sometimes faked or complicated by the odd lie. You can find records of these examinations, sometimes they have been printed or you may see the original document and they give a great deal of information, including details of parentage, family occupation and movement from place to place. From this detailed examination by the justices it would be determined which parish should be the correct parish of settlement and the person or sometimes the whole family could be issued with a settlement certificate for that parish or would be removed back to another parish. Again, the original removal order may be found or they may have been transcribed.

Up until 1795 the examinations were held before one or more Justices of the Peace on newcomers to the parish or to anyone thought likely to become a charge for their upkeep on the parish; after 1795 these persons had to be actually chargeable. A person or persons being examined would have to give details of age and place, information on apprenticeship or employment, date and place of marriage if relevant. Some people would already have a certificate from their parish of origin accepting liability if problems arose. Not many of these survive. If the magistrates were satisfied that another parish was the legal place of settlement, an order could be made to remove a pauper or a pauper and the family and a removal order was issued. This could lead to arguments as to who was actually responsible and families could be shifted between the two parishes, each eager to escape paying for the maintenance of the family or person involved.

It is of interest, for instance, in the Settlement and Removal orders in Derbyshire how many people were involved from outside of the county.

Thomas Parker who resides in Matlock a Hatter the son of James and Jane Parker was born in Hexham, Northumberland, he was apprenticed to his father and then to Joseph Turner in Alnwick, he then took off to find work in Ireland and eventually came to Matlock in 1834 and married in 1836 Jane by whom he has no children but she has one child Martha Walton. The assistant overseer John Else said Jane and child Martha were chargeable to Matlock as was Thomas Parker.

From Stepney Removals orders in 1831 there are examples: Mary Mail aged 27 and child passed from St Johns Hertford tried to appeal on the grounds upon settlement given by her late husband's grandfather. Appeal Order was squashed.

Betsey Marshall aged 12 passed from Bishopsgate upon a settlement of birth being illegitimate has 2 brothers now in the house also illegitimate admitted.

Sarah Smith and child and pregnant passed to Shadwell on her maiden settlement but found her husband's settlement was Shields the order cancelled passed to Shields. In 1757 John Thompson and his wife Mary from Tissington were removed to Rhye, Sussex.

Removal Orders
A number of these were concerned with young pregnant single girls removed to outside of the county in order to ensure they did not become a drain on the parish. Sometimes the order is suspended because the person has died or is too sick to be moved.

It was a very difficult problem as the cost of maintaining and running the parish grew – no parish wished to be landed with people for whom it felt it had no responsibility. On the other hand, how does a small parish feel and cope when it is face by the return of John Smith aged 72 unfit for any work, his 42 year old son another John Smith who has a sick wife and six children whose ages range from 15 months to 15?

In the Midlands and the north where there were in the late eighteenth and nineteenth centuries many thousands of migrants who flooded into the rapidly expanding industrial towns,

Settlement was not very fully covered or worried about and certificates were rarely issued, but in the southern half of England there is a sizeable collection of documents which have survived.

Vagrancy Records

Sometimes there is a Registration Book of Rogues and Vagabonds. They were usually found wandering and begging, often called Sturdy Beggars, and some of the examples show this to be appropriate. Early records do not always name women but in the following records this is not the case: Mary Parker widow with a child and she was whipped she was about the age of 30 proper of personage and she was able to quote the place of her birth being of Gravesend in Kent.

Another entry concerns Magdalen Payne who hid herself in Robert Cooper's barn between nine and ten o'clock of night one March evening, during the night in the extremity of pains of child bearing she cried out and Robert Cooper heard the noise. He poor man rather shaken no doubt ran for help and she was delivered of a woman child since christened Katherine. You might feel she had suffered enough, but, at the beginning of April she was taken before the Justice of the Peace Sir Henry Beckenham and confessed that she had long been a vagrant, whereupon Sir Henry ordered that she should be whipped until her body was bloodied. This sentence was carried out and later she was removed by the Constable from Beccles to Hitchin, a distance of some 75 miles or more.

Susannah Simpson was found wandering abroad in the open air in Derbyshire with her children Maria 9 and Elizabeth 13 months from the City of London.

In the 1750s the Constable had to carry two vagabonds on one horse and no night expenses were allowed unless the Constable travelled upward of 12 miles.

Children are noted: in 1772 John Johnson aged nine ran away from his father and mother about a month ago. John Higson when seven was apprenticed to Charles Price, Oxford Road London as a Chimneysweep, now aged seventeen found wandering in Derbyshire.

Another way of describing being homeless is given for Ann

Beresford: found lodging in the open air. In 1799 a potted biography showed how far her travels took her. Born in New York, America, when 21 she married George Watts, a soldier in the 57th Regiment of Foot. He was born in Stirling in Scotland. That about fifteen years hence she came to England with her husband, four years ago he left her in Ireland and has not been seen since. She was apprehended in Tideswell in Derbyshire.

Also: 1792 Thomas Collinson aged 16 born on board ship, the Culloden Man of War. Brought up in Shoreditch by his father in Peartree Court. Served John Hunter publican of the Thistle and Crown, Billiter Lane London. Then he was on board Salley Sloop, then he came back and lodged with his father James, next he went to James Skegg Publican at the Kings Head, Islington. He must have got fed up with that as we next find him selling pictures and books in Derbyshire where he is apprehended.

A surprising number of people when examined said they thought or believed or had no knowledge of where they were born. This applied to John Palmer, his wife Ann with their children Ann, Henry and Maria. They were apprehended in Portslade as rogues and vagabonds lying in outbuildings, wandering abroad and lodging in the open air.

Bastardy

Illegitimacy increased during the seventeenth and eighteenth centuries, and legally an illegitimate child was settled in the parish of its birth, not in that of either its father or mother as would have been the case were it legitimate. This was an incentive for the parish to try either to remove the mother before the birth or to find the putative father and his family and make them pay for the upkeep of the child or arrange a hasty marriage. The legal process usually began with an examination and the woman was required on oath to name the father and then he would, often together with his father, be asked to enter into a bond of indemnification by which upkeep would be paid, either in a lump sum or in weekly maintenance. It could happen, of course, that the father was a married man and there would be hell to pay. The language of some of the Bastardy Orders could be called quaint:

At Cuckfield in 1719 Mary Miles declares she is quick with child and that Isaac Pring of Linfield is the father.
In 1749 Sarah Beachey a single woman is now big with child.

In 1734 the grandmother has to pay: Ann Stapley a widow of Ardingly agreed to pay 9 pence a week for the keeping of a child lately born to her daughter Ann Stapley and who is now in the workhouse.

Another expression much used was "carnal knowledge of her body".

Bastardy bond against William King the Elder, collier and William King the younger, Carpenter in respect of Mary Wicks single woman who was delivered in all of three bastard children. Mary wicks has declared that William King is the father of the said children and he does admit and acknowledge this. William King the Elder having requested his son William King the Younger to join him in the bond and agrees to pay three shillings a week for maintenance. 6 Dec 1821

Hearth Tax

These are useful returns, but not many have survived and then rather raggedly. The parish Constable made the lists of those taxpayers between 1662 and 1689. They are useful as a guide to the size of houses people lived in. Persons with houses less than 20 shillings per annum were exempt, as of course was anyone who was on poor relief. For others, 2 shillings per hearth was payable and collected twice a year – at Michelmas and Lady Day. One hearth was relatively poor, three to four hearths of yeoman or gentleman status and six or more were rather grand. Other duties of the parish Constable (who was appointed by the Vestry) was to maintain the local prison and the stocks, to remove itinerant strangers, apprentice pauper children and he was also involved in training the local militia. It was not on the whole a popular job and the parishioner chosen often made sure he got out of it by paying someone else to do the job. There is a Gibson guide to the Hearth Tax and some County Record Offices have them and others can be found in the Quarter Session records.

Window Tax

This replaced the Hearth Tax. It was imposed in 1696 and abolished as late as 1851. It demanded the name and address of each taxpayer in England and Wales, and later in Scotland and Ireland, with the number of windows in a house. This told something of the status and economic situation of the owner. To avoid payment windows were boarded up. In 1825 all houses with fewer than eight windows were exempted. What records remain – and there are not many, with only a few names listed – will be found in the County Record Offices. Finding these records on the internet can be tricky as some counties appear to have put many of them online whereas at others you draw a blank, but it is well worth persevering. Also, Societies have transcribed the records and they are available on their publications sites.

From the foregoing you can see how much information can be found about our ancestors. Not just when they were hatched, matched and dispatched.

Chapter 6: Underused Sources of Genealogical Research in the UK

There are a number of sources of historical information which have not been exploited to their full potential by family historians.

The first such source is the CHURCHWARDEN'S PRESENTMENTS.

These were reports to the Bishop pertaining to the misdemeanours of the parishioners. They were also known more formally as Bills of Presentment.

The presentments relating to the parishioners cover a very broad range of offences, and may have details about your ancestors which cannot be found anywhere else. Be 'Street-wise' and look. One of the very useful characteristics of this information source is that people are named individually in these presentments.

Churchwardens of each parish were obliged to exhibit these Bills of Presentment to the ecclesiastical authorities, often at the Bishop's visitation. These records start quite early. Unfortunately, there is a blank period at the time of the Commonwealth, from 1649 to 1660. Their availability varies by county. For example, in Sussex, the earliest presentments are the Easter Bills of 1621. These were made less than 20 years after the Convocation of Canterbury in 1604. In this latter year there were actually 141 canons passed by the convocation and confirmed by royal letters patent. These regulations were the method by which presentments were made by the churchwardens, and they were rather far-reaching. The returns finish roughly in 1760.

The Churchwardens were quite important because there were quite a lot of rules covering their work. New Churchwardens were to be sworn in the week after Easter, and the outgoing Wardens had to make their presentments before the new Wardens took up their offices. Parish Clerks were also important because they kept a tally of all kinds of things that happened in the church such as baptisms, burials and marriages. The Parish Clerks were chosen by the incumbent and paid wages either at the hands of the Churchwardens or by their own collection.

There were also rules surrounding the selection and work of the Clerks. He should be at least 20 years of age, of honest conversation, able to read and write, of course, and if possible, able to sing. This last requirement may have created problems for some persons.

Some of the presentments dealt with repairs to the church. These can be quite amusing. There was one church in Upmarden in 1625 whose chancel was so full of pigeon dung and other filth that the parishioners had to hold their noses during services.

As I have mentioned, the presentments relating to parishioners cover a broad range of offences. These include not attending church on Sundays, neglecting to see that a mother is churched after her child's birth, making sure that children were baptized in infancy, ensuring that brawling, swearing and sexual immorality were kept under control, allowing shops and alehouses to stay open during services, non-payment of church rate, and acting without a licence as a school-master, physician, surgeon or midwife. Was one of your ancestors one of these?

As to individuals being named in these presentments we find, for example, the case of John Henderson. He decided that he would take advantage of a fine Sunday, the 15th July, 1621, to gather, tie and cock hay. There were other Sabbath-breakers, of course, such as Henry Parker, who was a constant player of nine pins. In these records there is the occasional mention of women – for example, Jane Harrod, who was presented as guilty of adultery for having a child while her husband was absent.

You also find the churchwardens not behaving as one would hope. There is the case of John Briggs, who in 1623 got drunk and lay all night in the street in Petworth. He did not learn his lesson, and a short time later he collapsed in a drunken state while walking uphill. The Vicars also were not always as well-behaved as they should have been. There is the example of John Woodcock, who was called upon in 1622 to bury a child, but was found to be "in drink" and incapable of officiating. And in Robert Johnson's time at Selsey, several children had died without benefit of baptism and several corpses had to be buried by the parish clerk for want of a minister. At Kirdford, the minister was presented for neglecting to bury the dead – corpses had to wait for four or five days before they were buried. If some of these gentlemen were this lax about their duties, one wonders about the quality and completeness of the material that was entered in the parish Registers. Many of the churchwarden's presentments have actually been transcribed. Ask at your County Record Office.

The second key and underused resource is the PROTESTATION OATHS OF 1641–42. These can be considered as one of the earliest forms of Census returns. The most important characteristic is that these returns cover the entire country. They are returns for all males over the age of 18 years who were in favour of the true Protestant religion. Also recorded were the names of those who were not in favour, but there were not very many of those. The names were recorded for each parish in each county and most of the surviving records are held at the House of Lords Record Office Library. Some of these have been transcribed and are held in the relevant County Record Office. Again, ask them.

The Protestation Oaths contain much useful information – the names of the overseers, the churchwardens, the ministers, and, as I suggested, you will sometimes find the names of the recusant papists. You will find out whether the men are householders or not, and absentees are also accounted for.

The Protestation Oaths were administered by the Justices of the Peace to the respective Ministers, to the Curates, the Constables, the Churchwardens and the Overseers. And these persons subsequently administered it to the male inhabitants of the parish. A good number of people signed with their mark, and one can find a variety of social ranks such as Esquire, Gentlemen or Master. Unfortunately, the trade of the individual was rarely recorded, but you can find a reference to an individual being the servant of another. Sometimes you are able to find something like "John Bloggs, senior", and "John Bloggs, junior", and there was one entry with three generations, with the second individual being identified as "middle".

It is wonderful from a genealogical point of view to find names on these protestation returns from such an early time. In one parish, Thomas Brown, William Hartley, and Thomas Simmons were very sick, and Edmond Ayling was too old and feeble to take the oath. There is a list in another parish of nine names of persons who were actually in London and were consequently said to be "out of warnings"- they obviously couldn't hear what was being said. There is a record of a Thomas Turner who "went to sea three weeks ago and has not yet returned". This is a very useful piece of genealogical information. In another parish, there was a list of five persons who were employed in the iron works, some miles away. These persons were apparently excused and not suspected of popery, for the main purpose of the oath was to support the Protestant religion and to find out who were the papists.

Several vicars made a report to the effect that there were no recusant papists in their parishes. And some Catholics appear to have taken the oath for reasons of self-preservation. But William Burgess of Angmering in West Sussex and James Drench, the alehouse keeper at Chichester, refused to take the oath. There is no indication of what happened to these men.

The number of names that you find on the returns is quite impressive. In one particular market town in Sussex, for instance, there are 509 names of men, ranging from the Gentlemen or Squires to the labourers. By contrast, in a small parish, there were as few as seven males named. But even here there was some useful information. William Jenman signed that he was under the age of 18 years, and there is an indication that Timothy Arnold was "dumb and speechless" and therefore exempt from the oath.

The protestation returns were the outcome of a resolution in the House of Commons made on the 30th July 1641, and it was quite extraordinary how swiftly and efficiently the whole operation was undertaken. It was actually carried out in a little more than six months. In some ways, these protestation returns can be looked upon as similar to the later Census returns. These early returns were valuable for containing males of all classes, for so often in earlier times it was only if you were rich or wicked that you left records. Very few women appear in the protestation returns, although there were a few widows who took the oath, especially in Lancashire.

Thirdly, do not overlook DIRECTORIES. These give excellent information to the family historian who is interested in forming a picture of the parish or village of their ancestors. These can be useful in tracking ancestors, but also as sources of information about the history and character of the region. Many are now available on the internet and you will find them as Historical Directories in the project undertaken by the University of Leicester, which covers a selection of directories from 1750 through to 1919 for England and Wales.

The following is an example of one of these descriptions, this one referring to a village in Surrey in the 1860s: "Woldingham is a parish and a small village in Surrey, four and a half miles south-east from Croydon and five miles from Godstone in the Tandridge and Godstone union." With this information, you know exactly where the village is located. You are told that the parish is found within the Bishopric of Winchester, and the Surrey Archdeaconry, if you are thinking of a will you need to prove. It gives you the name of the church – The Church of All Saints – and that the church consists of a nave, chancel and spire, and has only one bell. The description contains the information that the living of the vicarage is valued at 471 pounds per annum, and that the vicar was the Reverend John Dalton, M.A. There was also a chapel for the Wesleyan Methodists. The description contains the information that the parish contained exactly 1707 acres, and the population was 505 persons.

This directory continues with information about the lord of the manor, a dashing gentleman named Captain Atwood Dalton Wigrow. There is a parochial school erected jointly with the other two parishes, and it is supported by voluntary subscription. There is also a national school. There is a list of private residents, and a list of the commercial or tradespeople. You also find the name of the postmistress – Mrs. Fanny Book – and you are told that the letters arrive at 9 a.m., and if you want to send a letter, you have to have it there by 1:45 p.m. The nearest money order office is at Croydon. You are told that Mrs. Mary Ann Hunter is the School Mistress at the National School, and John Paul Symes is the Master of the Parochial School. The directory contains information about the carriers who make the trip to London – Luke Scott goes every Tuesday, returning that night, and John Constable goes every Thursday and returns on Friday. There is a list of the public houses – The White Lion, The Harrow, and The Leather Bottle. There is a list of the trades followed by the people of the parish – tailor, miller, wheelwright, blacksmith, butcher, farrier, bricklayer, fruit grower, baker and grocer, not forgetting the farmers of the parish.

All in all, this gives you a complete snapshot of life, and they are quite remarkable in the detail.

One of the earliest directories is *Gore's Directory of Liverpool* in 1766, and one of the most useful is *Holden's Triennial Directory* of 85 provincial towns in Ireland and Great Britain, 1805–7. The list includes Dublin, Cork, Waterford and Belfast, Edinburgh, Glasgow, and Paisley, plus all the other big towns in England and Wales. For the same date, there is *Holden's Triennial Directory for London*, which contains upward of 140,000 names. These Directories give excellent information to the family historian who is interested in forming a picture of the parish or village of their ancestors. They can be useful in tracking ancestors, but also as sources of information about the history and character of the region.

Fourthly, MANORIAL RECORDS, which are another source of genealogical information, are often overlooked. In this regard there is a very good reference book called *Manorial Records* by Professor Paul Harvey published by the British Records Association. These records are old, and this is an important characteristic to remember. From the time of the Norman Conquest until well into the seventeenth and eighteenth centuries, the manorial system shaped the framework of the lives of most of the rural population in England and much of Wales. And even after the decline in the importance of the system from the seventeenth century, they continued to function as the only means by which copyhold land was transferred. And so these records, if they survive, hold a great fund of genealogical information.

Manorial records are defined, in manorial document rules, as court rolls, surveys, maps, documents, and books of every description relating to boundaries, wastes, customs or courts of the manor. It must be remembered that the manorial system did not encompass all of the land in England and Wales – in England, some land was never subjected to manorial jurisdiction, whilst in Wales, it was never particularly widespread. In addition, one of the snags of the use of these records is that mediaeval manorial records were almost always written in Latin and relied heavily on abbreviations, although English comes much more into use in the beginning of the seventeenth century. After 1733, thankfully for most of us, parliament decreed that all administrative records should be written in English.

In coming to understand manorial records, it is important to understand the concept of a "manor". *The Surveyor's Dialogue,* published as early as 1607, defined a manor as "A Little Commonwealth", where the tenants are the members, the lands are the bulks, and the lord is the head. Manor records are very useful, especially if you are trying to trace the ownership of property. The pattern of land ownership and use was fairly constant up until the Black Death in 1349, when the pattern did change because tenants, being in shorter supply, were able to bargain for their land and make demands for greater security in the form of deeds and conditions. Eventually, of course, many tenants became known as "customary tenants" because they were said to hold their land "by custom". Later, there were mainly two types of manorial tenure – freehold and customary hold. There was a third, less frequent type – tenure by lease.

The Manorial Documents Register is maintained by the National Archives on behalf of the Master of the Rolls and it is not a register of title. For that you need the sections of the Manorial Documents Register which can be searched on line. This includes a list of the counties covered, for instance, Surrey. Any not covered have been microfilmed and can be searched at the TNA. They are particularly useful when your family research approaches the early eighteenth century and the later decades of the seventeenth century as records become more sparse and do not give much detailed information. For example, as shown in early baptisms where in some Parish Registers the entry often refers only to John son of John Curtis.

Fifthly, CORONER's REPORTS. Family historians tend to get fairly excited about the value of coroner's reports. People see in the burial record that the person was buried by coroner's warrant. But these records have a really low survival rate. There is a *Gibson Guide* to what is available, but if you have someone who was buried by coroner's warrant, it is much more useful to look in the local newspaper for a report of the coroner's record. Newspapers often give more details, and the coroner's report itself is unlikely to have survived. I have a couple of examples of coroner's reports, which did survive.

The first refers to John Shark, who died by excessive drinking, in October of 1779. Another is that of Elizabeth Leonard who apparently died after falling from her chair, she being alone and much intoxicated by liquor at the time. Another relates the story of a child of two years who died after drinking boiling hot water from a kettle. And there was Mary Greenfield, who died in August of 1806 of natural causes accelerated by the neglect of her husband, James. Rose Edwards apparently died after drinking hemlock tea. Anne Pentacost died accidentally after taking opium incautiously, apparently administered instead of rhubarb! One wonders about the nature of the kitchen when opium can accidentally be substituted for rhubarb! Among the surviving coroner's reports, there are quite a few cases of children dying after accidentally coming in contact with boiling water. In general, if they survive, coroner's reports can be quite enlightening, but newspaper reports should be checked as well.

Sixthly, another genealogical source which is quite useful, especially if you are trying to keep track of somebody, relates to the GAMEKEEPER'S DEPUTATIONS. These records also give the names of the manors during the eighteenth and nineteenth centuries, a period when it is quite difficult to trace lordships. These Gamekeepers Deputations start quite early, originating from a statute of 1710 under which the appointments were to be registered with the clerk of the peace for the county. Their survival rate is reasonable. These records have been indexed in some counties, greatly facilitating their use. Again check with your local record office.

In Sussex, for example, these deputations begin in 1781, and continue until the late 1890s. In my opinion, these records are quite valuable because one didn't have to be a gamekeeper to be deputed. The gamekeepers are recorded as often as menial servants or labourers, although a large proportion are of high standing. The deputations are divided into five entries – the date of the deputation, the name of the landowner, the estates which are covered, the name of the gamekeeper, and the date of the issuance of the certificate. It appears that deputations could be made and allowed to accumulate and then all returned on the same day. These records produce a particularly good source for family history, as it gives you the names of the labourers and where they could be living – all information which is not readily available from other sources.

The records have the following form: *I, Harry Winton, of Sompting, in the County of Sussex, Gentleman, Lord of the Manor of Cokeham by virtue of several Acts of Parliament made for the preservation of game, have deputed, constituted and appointed Richard Witpane, labourer, of Lancing, in the said County of Sussex, to be my Gamekeeper, dated the 12th of July, 1807.*

Many of the people who deputed the gamekeepers, of course, held many manors, such as the Duke of Norfolk, who held well over 20 manors in Sussex alone. The occupations of the gamekeepers included yeoman, husbandman, weavers, carpenters, victuallers, labourers, servants and butchers – a very wide cross-section of the community. And a very good feature of these records is that they are yearly records, so that you may be able to trace the movements of a labourer for several years. I was very interested to find one family who served in this capacity from 1802 until the late 1860s. During this period of time, the family moved a distance of some 70 miles. Apart from these Deputations, it would have been very difficult to follow the track of this family.

We come to the seventh category. Here is a somewhat rarefied source of information: the INQUISITIONS POST-MORTEM. These date from as early as 1485, and end in 1660. There are several series and they are held at the National Archives at Kew, although it may be that the County Record Office has transcribed a copy of those that pertain to a particular area. If a person held land which belonged to the crown, then, upon his death, an inquiry was held into his possessions, services due, and his rightful heirs. So you can see that these records give quite a bit of useful genealogical information at an early date. There are basically five pieces of information – the name of the deceased, the location of the inquisition, the date of death, the name and relationship of the heir, and a short description of the property, including wills, grants and marriage settlements affecting it. If it is transcribed completely, you get the name of the escheator (or official before whom the inquisition was held), the names of the jurors, the acreage and the value of the lands, and the names of the manors affected. This is an item of great value if you are trying to trace property.

One example refers to John Brown of Chichester, April 3, 34 Elizabeth (the 34th year of the reign of Queen Elizabeth I), his heir being his son John, aged 28. The record tells you about the lands – Brian's land (alias Milland), and Luca's land in West Hoathly in Sussex. It also tells you that Joan Brown is the widow of John Brown, and that she is living and takes the rents and the profits.

Another, more complicated example – Elizabeth Gaston, aged 40 years, whose heir is George Gaston, of Balkan, brother of William Gaston, father of Elizabeth. The inquisition was held at a place called East Grinstead (eight miles from Balkan), on the 22nd January, in the eighth year of the reign of Queen Elizabeth. There were actually 15 jurors, including a father and son – and they are named. The story that this record reveals is quite a sad one, in that apparently Elizabeth Gaston had been, from birth, "an idiot, of weak mind, so that she cannot control her affairs". She does not know the lands she has, or whom the land was held from. The record does not contain the judgement so one is left to wonder whether George Gaston managed to gain control of the land.

A third example concerns William Brown of Petworth, a clothier. The inquisition was held on the 30th June, in the 7th year of the reign of Edward VI. In this inquisition, there was quite a long description of the land and about some person who was outlawed for burglary and felony for having taken some goods. In general, if you are fortunate to trace your family history back to the seventeenth, sixteenth and fifteenth centuries, then you will find that there are indeed still some interesting records which you can use.

Then there are the RECORDS OF CHARITIES. The Street-wise enquirer should see Herbert Fry's *Royal Guide to the London Charities* published in 1917. The format is the name of the institution when founded and where situated. Some examples: St. Marylebone Female Protection Society; 1838; 157–9, Marylebone Road, N.W. This institution was established for the purpose of affording a home for young women between the ages of 14 and 30 who have fallen from the path of virtue and are about to become mothers – but who up to the time of their fall had borne a good character. The London Female Guardian Society; 1807; 191 High St., Stoke Newington, N.; To provide an asylum for the rescue, reclamation and protection of betrayed and fallen women and to train them for domestic service. The inmates receive the benefits of the Charity for not less than eighteen months. The Master Bakers' Pension and Almshouse Society, London; 1832, Almshouses at Le Bridge Road; to provide homes and pension in and out of doors for aged and decayed master bakers or the widows of such.

All kinds of people were involved in this sector. For example, the author Lewis Carroll gave to many charities. He made regular payments on the 1st January and he must have taken an interest as to how a charity performed as the list varied from year to year with some charities being removed and other added. They included The Governesses Benevolent Association opened in 1843 which provided homes and annuities for governesses left destitute or too old to work and The Dogs Temporary Home which started in 1860 and was later moved to Battersea.

We all use printed sources. One important printed source not to be overlooked is *The Gentleman's Magazine*. Founded in London in 1731 by Edward Cave, it was published until 1922. It contains local history, geographical details and family history which includes birth, marriages and deaths, promotions in the Services and also entries from America. It is available on Ancestry to 1868.

Worth googling, too, are local history sites, including war memorials which can give more information than the War Graves Commission site. The Old Bailey records, too, do not just cover the accused but also witnesses. I found my great grandfather Dr. Bewley giving evidence in a murder trial there.

The records of *Hospital and Lunatic Asylums* are closed for 75 or a hundred years, but with the Freedom of Information Act if a direct relative is identified these records can be obtained.

Then there are the many indexes on all manner of relevant topics which are immensely valuable to genealogists. Indexes have been produced for brass-workers, for brick-makers, for brush-makers, for comb-makers, about shoe-makers, about masons. There is an index for the canal boat people, and this is very useful because these people were constantly in motion. The index of comb-makers is particularly interesting because it contains quite a number of Huguenots who came over with the trade of comb-making.

The British Newspaper Archive website gives access to over 6 million fully searchable pages, featuring more than 200 newspaper titles from every part of the UK and Ireland. A further 2 million pages will be added over the first two years of the project, with 8,000 new pages every day.

These newspapers – which mainly date from the nineteenth

century, but which include runs dating back to the first half of the eighteenth century – cover every aspect of local, regional and national news. This new resource is published and managed by brightsolid, in collaboration with the British Library.

So there are these major sources which should not be overlooked. It is Street-wise to study them.

Chapter 7: Kill or Cure? Medicines and Illness in the 19th Century

How did your ancestors live and die? And how do we know? What diseases did they suffer from, and what records do we have? Family historians are usually interested in the health and disease issues which confronted their ancestors and this also makes one wonder what illnesses we are going to inherit. There are many aspects to this subject, and I will try and cover a number of these.

Before the introduction of death certificates on 1st July 1837, the main sources of information on the causes of death were the Bills of Mortality which date back to the sixteenth century. These are not, of course, always reliable and they were usually only compiled for the larger cities. The original Bill for Registration of Births and Deaths in 1836 did not provide for the cause of death to be included in the registration procedure. The medical profession was anxious that the cause of death should be stated, and pressure also came from that remarkable man, Edwin Chadwick, who was Secretary for the Poor Law Commission at the time. Support also came from other sources, particularly proponents of sanitary reform, which was emerging as a significant issue given the rapid growth in the urban population. These persons persuaded the House of Lords to introduce an amendment to the Bill to have the cause of death added to the death certificate. Fortunately for us, the Bill was passed in this amended form.

In practice, it was rare for a doctor to be called to the presence of a dying person, and the informant who was providing information for the registration of the death could only guess as to the cause of death. Some conditions such as smallpox, cholera or typhoid would have been fairly obvious, but the informant could only guess in many cases. The Registrar had no alternative but to accept the information which came from the informant who was registering the death.

Some of the official causes of death which appeared on the death certificates in the middle of the nineteenth century were more than a little bit strange. There was something called Black Thrush, and also Black Jaundice. (I had some nasty personal experience with Yellow Jaundice – it is not hard to believe that something called Black Jaundice could kill someone.) There was also something called Stoppage (which sounds quite unpleasant) and leads to the question of whereabouts, and also the very vague "Visitation of God" (it would be difficult to argue with that).

Then there are deaths which were labelled as "Decline" and "Weakness". A man from Brighton was said to have died from "Indiscreet Bathing", and a man in Cardiff was said to have suffered for four years and finally succumbed to "The King's Evil". (Since Queen Victoria had been on the throne for some time, this disease should have been re-named "The Queen's Evil".) There were also large numbers of deaths from the common childhood diseases of convulsions, measles, chicken pox, whooping cough, scarlet fever and diphtheria together with many incidents of children being scalded or in some way being burnt to death. There were also epidemics of smallpox and great pox, the latter of which presumably was more serious.

I myself was part of the smallpox epidemic which struck the city of Brighton in the winter of 1950–51. At this time, Brighton was very much dependent on the holiday-makers for its economy, and there was an interest in down-playing the significance of this event so as not to discourage the summer visitors. Local newspapers at that time just gave a dozen lines to the outbreak. There was a similar situation one hundred years earlier when cholera struck Brighton in 1849. Not wanting to draw unnecessary attention to the surplus of deaths, the Registrar used a small cross instead of using the word "cholera", which might have reduced the number of visitors to the town – which is now a city.

The transmissible nature of diseases was recognized only late in the nineteenth century. A classic example of this was that of puerperal sepsis or fever following the birth of a child. Mothers were very vulnerable at this moment in time – washing and scrubbing-up was rarely employed and basic hygiene was quite poor, so infection of the womb was usually contracted during or immediately after the birth. Acute leukaemia was not properly diagnosed because no connection was made between lumps and bumps and cancer. The causes of weakness and lethargy were not well understood because the nutritional disorders were not recognized, nor the importance of vitamins and minerals, the lack of which could lead to rickets when the bones softened. The recognition of tumours and the existence of and cellular nature of dementia had to await the arrival of more powerful microscopes and brain microscopy in the twentieth century.

We know of Baker's Cyst, Huntingdon's Disease, Bell's Palsy and Sydenham's Chorea (St Vitus Dance) – a disease affecting children with rheumatic fever and characterised by jerky uncontrollable movements. But naming of some diseases had an amusing aspect. A skin disorder was discovered in Hungary by a man by the name of Cohen in the late nineteenth century. The normal process would have been for the doctor to attach his name to this disorder, but Mr. Cohen chose the maiden name of his wife in order to give the condition a more impressive title. In this way, Kopopsky's sarcoma was identified. Joseph Toynbee was a leading ear specialist in the 1860s who came to an unfortunate end when he tried to prove that tinnitus could be improved by inhaling a combination of hydrogen cyanide and chloroform and then holding his nose. He was also an ancestor of the journalist Polly Toynbee. Sir James Paget was a surgeon and pathologist who had three diseases named after him. An exceptional man, he was appointed in 1858 as Surgeon Extraordinary to Queen Victoria. In 1871 he nearly died from an infection picked up whilst carrying out a post-mortem examination. Having survived, he eventually died in 1899 aged 95. Salmonella was named after Daniel Elmer Salmon, an American Veterinary Pathologist with the American Department of Agriculture. He had been orphaned at the age of eight and was raised by his second cousin Aaron Howell Salmon, who had a farm. Credit does not always go to where it is due, as it was Daniel's assistant Theobald Smith who discovered the cause, but it was named in honour of Daniel. Bell's Palsy came from Sir Charles Bell, a Scottish surgeon in 1829, and Parkinson's from James Parkinson – an English doctor who as early as 1817 published an essay on shaking Palsy.

Another disorder which was very poorly recognized and defined was motor-neuron disease. The mother of a friend of mine died recently of this illness. When she examined the death registrations of several generations of her mother's family she found several references to different forms of paralysis, General, Total, Partial, Creeping, confirming the influence of genetics in its distribution and the fact that this condition was a significant cause of death before it was officially identified and labelled. Another instance of this is Telegraphic Paralysis, which affected Telegraph Clerks when they found over time that their hands would become cramped, then the thumb, next the first and second finger and finally the wrist – the forerunner of Repetitive Strain Injury perhaps. An interesting point arose when a photograph of a great grandmother showed her with twisted and deformed hands from rheumatoid arthritis and her grandchild in later life in her photograph showed exactly the same hands.

One reason that the profile of the causes of death today is different than it was one hundred years ago is because our ancestors did not live long enough to die of the diseases that we see today. Evidence of this would come from a search of the surname index of 1881 or 91 for a common name like William Smith.

One would not find all that many people over the age of 60, with correspondingly smaller numbers over 70 and over 80. Thus, the diseases which affect us in our older ages, like the cancers and heart disease, were not as common in the earlier period. In the nineteenth century it was not always usual to have three generations of a family alive at the same time, when today it is relatively common to have four generations, if not five, living at the same time. As another reflection of this change, the expectation of life in 1841 was 40 years for men and 42 years for women. Many women would not have experienced the change of life or have had to ponder the pros and cons of HRT Treatment.

Apart from smallpox, the other major infectious disease of the nineteenth century was cholera. There were three very bad outbreaks of cholera in London in the 1830s. In one year in this decade 40,000 burials took place in London. These epidemics and resulting deaths put great pressure on the existing cemeteries and led to the establishment of some of our large cemeteries such as Highgate, Kensal Green, Abney Park and others. Those known as the Magnificent Seven garden cemeteries are: All Souls, Kensal Green (opened 1833); South Metropolitan Cemetery, West Norwood (1837); St. James, Highgate (1839); Abney Park (1840); West of London and Westminster Cemetery, Brompton (1840); All Saints, Nunhead (1840), City of London and Tower Hamlets, Tower Hamlets (1841). And, of course, Brookwood (1854).

It was not until the outbreak of 1854 that the origin and spread of cholera came to be better understood, and this was because of the work of Dr. John Snow and Dr. William Farr. These two men found the answer to the spread of this disease. Dr. Farr was born in 1807 in Shropshire and was the son of a farm labourer. William Farr's intelligence was recognized by the local squire and he was given a basic education. In his will, the squire left some money for William Farr to allow him to further his education at the University of Paris and at the University College in London. This was quite an unusual career path in the early nineteenth century. Dr. Farr was appointed by the General Registry Office in 1839 as the Compiler of Abstracts and later as the Statistical Superintendent.

Oddly enough, Dr. Snow, too, had come from humble origins, being the eldest of nine children when he was born in 1813 in York. His father was a labourer and they lived in Micklegate, an area which was very unsanitary. It is possible that his early experiences with contaminated water may have laid the foundation for part of his research and discoveries. Dr. Snow and Dr. Farr were working together when the cholera epidemic of 1854 occurred. As part of their work to explain the spread of cholera through the population, these two doctors noted the occupations and residences of the afflicted persons. One interesting death had occurred on September 2nd. It was the death of a Mrs. Susannah Ealey, a resident of Hampstead, a community on the northern edge of the city and so considered to be healthy because of its elevation. After closer investigation, the doctors discovered that Mrs. Ealey regularly sent her footman to fetch a bottle of water from the Broad Street pump. Mrs. Ealey fell ill and died within two days of drinking the water, as did her niece who was visiting her at the time from Islington, another community thought to be healthy because of its elevation. With this information, the doctors discovered that the spring which supplied the Broad Street pump was severely contaminated with cholera. The water companies which supplied the water were also thought to be culprits in this affair.

When cholera returned to London in 1866, the number of deaths was relatively low except in the east end of London. Dr. Farr suggested that the East London Water Company was responsible for the delivery of contaminated water. The company denied any culpability, but it was later discovered that the company, in responding to a summer drought, had transferred water from a condemned open reservoir near the heavily polluted River Lea. So

Dr. Farr was fully justified in his accusations.

The remainder of Dr. Farr's career was rather unfortunate. Upon the retirement of George Graham, the Registrar-General in 1879, Dr. Farr was thought to be in the running to be the replacement. But much to his disappointment, the position went to someone else, and this event led to Dr. Farr's retirement. Dr. Snow however continued his remarkable career, promoting the use of statistics to establish the link between disease and social conditions. He worked with Florence Nightingale, and went on to prove the connection between hydrophobia and rabid dogs. All in all, an impressive career.

Sir Humphrey Davy, who was born in 1778, was the inventor of the miner's safety lamp, and also discovered the properties of nitrous oxide, namely that when it was inhaled it first produced euphoria, leading to uncontrollable laughter and sobbing and then effectively passing out. He immediately called it laughing gas. But there was a problem with nitrous oxide in that the effects did not last long and thus it was unsuitable for medical operations. In 1844 an American dentist called Horace Wells attended a demonstration in Hartford, Connecticut, about nitrous oxide and Wells had the idea of using it for pain relief by gas inhalation, reviving the thoughts of Humphrey Davy some years earlier.

Then there was the introduction of chloroform, first used by Dr. James Simpson the well-known Edinburgh gynaecologist in 1847, at his house in Gower Street, in Central London. He used it by sprinkling it on a handkerchief which was then placed over the patient's nose and mouth so that they could inhale the vapour. In 1853 it was used by Queen Victoria for the birth of her eighth child, Prince Leopold, and she was delighted with the experience. There was one woman who does seem to have been over-grateful for the pain-free delivery, as in the birth indexes in 1903 the child is registered as Anaesthesia Leech.

Unfortunately, it was not always possible to administer an anaesthetic, as shown in a hospital record for William Welfare, aged 55, a Labourer from Wivelsfield in Sussex. His clothes had been caught in a threshing machine. By the time he had been brought to the hospital (a distance of some 15 miles), he was nearly exhausted by hemmorrage (*sic*) and an amputation was needed without delay. When he was put on the operating table he was so low and his circulation so feeble that chloroform was not admissible, so that before the amputation could take place – and as it proceeded – they dosed him with half a pint of brandy during which time it was observed he was almost moribund. He survived for fourteen days and then sadly he had another haemorrhage and died.

Vaccination against smallpox caused much controversy during the nineteenth century. The first Vaccination Act was in 1840 and this allowed free vaccination to poor people. In 1853 Vaccination was made compulsory in the first three months of a baby's life, and evasion by parents could lead to a fine or imprisonment. In 1867 the Act was applied more stringently and the compulsion was increased to include those aged 14. This change was followed by a similarly stringent 1871 Act. In 1898 that Act was amended to allow exemption to parents based on conscience. Many people were against vaccination and the Anti-Vaccination League was formed. Apart from the imposition of fines and imprisonment, houses and schools could also be searched to find unvaccinated children. And when the parents were summoned before the Justices they were rarely given the opportunity to justify themselves or give reasons why they had not complied with the Act. Perhaps your ancestors may have been among them?

There was the odd case of a Mr. Charles Nye from Kent who, having lost two children from the effects (as he thought) of vaccination, refused to allow his other children to be vaccinated. Between 1869 and 1881 he was served with no less than thirteen summonses. Each time he was fined and these were always unpaid; on five occasions he was sent to prison. During one of his incarcerations the authorities attempted to vaccinate him but such a row erupted and Mr. Nye became so angry and said that he felt murderous towards the Doctor so much so that the Doctor took flight and the warders were called to return Mr. Nye to his cell. Prisoners had to be vaccinated if not previously done and after they were weighed they would be taken to the infirmary where one man of some considerable bulk was actually injected in both arms.

One of the most important social changes was related to the increase in the population. In 1800, it is reckoned that the population of England and Wales stood at 9 million, although then few had an accurate idea of the extent to the population. By 1841, the population stood at almost 16 million, and had reached

36 million by 1911. When one considers the task of building the public health infrastructure for this larger population, it must have been a tremendous labour.

There was chronic over-crowding and many people died of diseases which are commonly prevented and cured today. There is the classic case of the "creaking gate" people who were afflicted with a heart condition and who spent their time resting while others ran around taking care of them. These "creaking gate" people often went on to outlive their loved ones.

There are good records from hospitals. And from these records, you may be able to find a physical description of your ancestors, something which is rarely available from other sources. I had occasion to look into the records of a hospital which opened in 1826 and I examined records from 1843 to 1845 to gain an impression of the medical conditions which prompted our ancestors to seek medical attention. The first patient that I found was a day labourer by the name of Thomas Barfoot. He was 38 years of age and admitted on 28th December 1843. He was extremely emaciated and so weak as to be totally unable to help himself. He had been brought to the hospital from a Union Workhouse, a trip which took two and a half days. Upon arrival at the hospital, his chief complaint was with the muscles of his neck and the posterior part of the head. The pain was so bad that he begged to have his neck cut open. The hospital staff started treatment – fermentations, anodyne poultices, belladonna poultices, followed by leeches and blisters – but without success. His pain persisted. By the eighteenth day, he complained of being completely unable to swallow and observation of his throat was impossible because of problems in opening his mouth. He requested that his head be thrown back every two or three minutes because this greatly aided him to breathe. The situation was getting rather desperate. On the nineteenth day, the doctor decided that a tracheotomy was required to prevent suffocation. After the operation, the patient described himself as "relieved", but immediately after this statement he blanched, threw back his head and expired. After the death of this patient, there was a post-mortem examination with very detailed findings. He probably had lockjaw, or tetanus.

The other disease which is creeping back to occupy a position of considerable importance today, especially in the larger cities in Great Britain, is consumption or tuberculosis. I feel quite strongly about TB, having lost so many of my own great uncles and aunts to this disease. Eight out of eleven children died before they were 18 years of age because of it. They lived in the smoky east end of London. The difference now is that there is effective treatment for this condition.

There is then the question of people being able to eat properly. Mouth hygiene was often primitive. Many needed replacements for their lost teeth, and many second-hand teeth came from mortuaries, dissecting rooms and the gallows. The people who supplied the teeth were known as "resurrectionists". Some only took teeth but some took bodies too. Astley Cooper was one of the most popular dentists in nineteenth-century London. He kept many people employed as he needed a constant supply of teeth in his profession. It is ironic that at the end of the nineteenth century when men were needed for the army at the outbreak of the Boer War, they were found to be undernourished, some with rickets and generally unfit for active service. Now a hundred years later with the abundance of junk food and lack of exercise the very opposite of this problem needs to be solved.

Sexually-transmitted diseases were another serious issue. The story of Lord Randolph Churchill, Winston's father, is well known. Another case is the very sad birth and then death certificate of little Not Wanted James Colvill, born in 1861 and who died a few months later. He may have been caused by syphilis being passed down. Once I was delivering a presentation when I realized that I was about to describe an ancestor of one of the members of the audience in terms which were not totally flattering. It was too late to turn back. I related that Hannah Monnery, aged 22, was "of scrofulous appearance, and one of six children who lived with their father and mother who were also of an unhealthy constitution". The descendant in the audience seemed to be pleased to have any information about her missing ancestor.

These medical records contain some items of detailed biographical information. You should search for the good and the bad. I found a Mary Newland, aged 29, "healthy-looking, dark hair, [whose] last confinement was seven years ago, complains of impaired power motion of left leg, gradually coming on for last four and a half years." She was married, and the ceremony had taken place at Basingstoke. She had had three children. Her condition started after the first child and worsened with her third delivery. She wasn't able to walk without holding on to something. She was a patient for two months and was released with no improvement.

Death certificates of the twentieth century contain much more precise diagnostic information about a death. They provide the name of the person who has died, as well as the date and place of death. One I found from 1938 listed cardiac failure, cellulite of the abdomen and an enlarged prostate. A certificate from 1967 contains the term "myocardial degeneration", both of these gentlemen being over 60 years of age. One particular gentleman was just about 87 years of age, and the death certificate gives his occupation, where he died, of course, the name and address of his informant, and then four causes of death. In this case the certificate lists bronchial-pneumonia, chronic bronchitis, a recumbency due to age at infirmity, and finally a benign prostatic enlargement.

Over the time period which we have just considered one can see the increasing definition of the causes of death, going from the poorly defined "Decay of Nature" to four separate conditions. On the death certificate of a 7 month old baby who died in 1899 in Doncaster the cause of death was given as Marasmus. This was a condition which was unknown to me and I was shocked to find that it was Severe Malnutrition, which affects more than 50 million children worldwide today, with many cases in Africa and India. When we see on the television starving children in third-world countries this was probably what this baby in Doncaster looked like. The family are on the Census returns; they did not seem to be a particularly poor family and the father was employed in a trade.

There were also diseases associated with particular trades. I am not sure if anyone now suffers from Scrivener's Palsy or Grocer's Itch, from the mites found in the handling of flour and sugar, or Weaver's Bottom or Potter's Rot, which was so known because the dust caused the potter's lungs to rot. Or Bagpiper's Fungus because the bagpipes were traditionally made from sheepskin, and when the inside was coated with treacle or honey to keep them airtight they were a breeding ground for spores and fungus, Railway passengers in railway accidents which were said to involve the spine were described as post-traumatic symptoms, which led to claims for damages although there were no visible signs of injury. It became so controversial that a book was written by John Eric Erichsens and it was called Erichsensdisease. Were these early cases of what is now known as whiplash?

Famously, Charles Dickens was involved in the Staplehurst rail crash near Headcorn in Kent when there was a derailment at Staplehurst on 9th June 1865. The South Eastern Railway Folkestone to London boat train derailed while crossing a viaduct where a length of track had been removed during engineering works. The crash killed ten and injured 40 passengers.

The novelist was travelling with his mistress Ellen Ternan and her mother on the train. They all survived the derailment and Dickens got down from the carriages and tended the victims, some of whom died while he was with them. This traumatic and shocking experience affected Dickens greatly. He lost his voice for two weeks and afterwards was always nervous when travelling by train. He used alternative means of travel when he could. He died five years to the day after the accident, and his son said that he had never fully recovered.

The Street-wise enquirer will want to examine as many relevant medical records as they can find – hospital records, asylum records, and Workhouse records. It is always worth thinking about death certificates, which tell us much. If you are fortunate, when you get into the Parish Registers, you may also have a parish incumbent who was good about putting down the causes of death.

You may have medical staff in your own family tree. Medical journals, too, often printed obituaries, as does *the British Medical Journal*, for example, today. Well worth a look.

Chapter 8: Baby Farming

This is a sad and macabre topic, but one of which the Street-wise enquirer needs to be aware. Perhaps there is such a tale in their background? The information that we have from the surviving records of what went on is deeply shocking.

The protection of infant lives was a very real issue in the nineteenth century. There were more vigilant laws against the mistreatment of animals, and even stricter laws for cow keepers, than for the protection of infants until then. In 1874 there was a Parliamentary Select Committee report with the very same title: the Protection of Infant Life. The Committee of seventeen people sat from May 1871 and took evidence from a variety of professional people.

They included Dr. William Farr (head of the statistical department of the General Registry Office since 1838), Mr. John Bowring (clerk to the Guardians of the City of London Union), Mr. Charles Cameron (the editor of the *North British Daily Mail*), Mrs. Jane Dean Main (the Superintendent of the Refuge for Deserted Mothers and Children at Great Coram Street), Mrs. Susannah Meredith (Treasurer of the Female Prisoners Aid Society), Mr. Ernest Hart (a surgeon and Editor of the *British Medical Journal*) and another Surgeon, Mr. John Brendan Curgeven (who was also Honorary Secretary to the Infant Life Protection Society which was established in 1870). Another very important witness was Sergeant Relf of the Metropolitan Police. We will see his detailed evidence, below.

The minutes of the committee are lengthy but they make fascinating reading. One of the conclusions they reached was that there were two classes of baby farming. Firstly, the children who were put out for hire with the deliberate knowledge and possibly the intention that they would die very quickly. And, secondly, children put out either in the daytime or by the week by the mother to enable them to carry on their casual or usual employment.

Matters in London were brought to a head in 1870 by the trials of two women, Margaret Waters and Mary Hall. According to the evidence put to the Select Committee, there were a large number of private houses used in London as lying-in establishments for confinements. Very few of the infants born in these places were taken away by their natural mothers. They were usually left behind to be fostered or adopted and the owner of the establishment would receive payment relevant to the means of the mother for their services. The sum of money could range from £5 to £50 or even £100, and the baby would then be taken away, generally immediately after birth, often to the worst kind of baby farming house. Those women in their turn were remunerated by a small sum of money, totally inadequate for the permanent maintenance of the baby. And so it was obviously much more profitable for the baby farmer to be rid of the baby as soon as possible, pocket the difference and take on the next baby or babies, of which there was always a plentiful supply. It was comparatively simple to be rid of babies after they were born.

Most of the "farmed" babies were illegitimate and their births had not been registered. Nobody really, except the owners of the establishments involved, knew much about them and I doubt if some of them knew anything except that it was a baby and that it was a source of income. Mothers rarely came to visit and even if they did and they were not happy with the circumstances they had very few other alternatives for where to place the baby. Often babies would be buried by baby farmers as still-births.

Pauper children born in the Workhouse were actually more fortunate in some ways, for they remained with their mother until they chose to discharge themselves, sometimes quite shortly after the birth. Orphaned and deserted children were kept in the Workhouse until two years of age and then they were usually boarded out.

"Baby farming", as it was known, was widespread in London and some other large towns both in England and Scotland. But it was in London and its neighbourhood that it was largely done with criminal intent. In the manufacturing towns in Yorkshire and Lancashire this appeared not to have been the case, and the mortality of children put out to nurse was mainly through carelessness and not intentional. In Manchester the coroner stated that since 1838 only one case of baby farming had been brought to his attention.

The basic intention of the professional baby farmer was to solicit as many sickly infants as possible, usually under the age of three months because life was so dangerous for them anyway that their deaths would appear more natural. They would adopt the baby for a set fee and then hasten their demise in order to make the most profit. The babies were dosed with laudanum and fed watered-down milk – sometimes laced with lime. They would die quickly from malnutrition, and any cost of burial was avoided by wrapping the naked bodies of the dead infants in newspapers and dumping them in a deserted place or by throwing them into the Thames.

Older infants were also taken in and sometimes they were more lucrative, because they were more robust and healthy and their mothers would struggle to support them. They suffered a worse death because they died from slow starvation as the mothers continued to pay the weekly fees demanded from the baby farmer. For older children neglect, abuse and hunger were a way of life. One such was little Frederick John Wood, a sickly 14 month old who was farmed out to a Mrs. Savill of 24 Swayton Road, Bow in East London. His mother visited him every week, thinking that he was being well cared for. Ten months later he died and it was found that he had died from fluid on the brain, that he had a malformed chest and that his hip had been broken for some time. When questioned, Mrs. Savill admitted that while taking Frederick upstairs to bed she had stumbled and fallen on the boy. Though the child cried she simply put him to bed in an egg-crate filled with straw, a crate so narrow that he could not turn over. At the time of little Frederick's death she had eleven children in her care and five had already died. Based on Dr. Atkins' testimony – who said that the boy had died of natural causes – the jury had little option but to return a verdict of not guilty. But they were not happy about this and asked that a censure against Mrs. Savill be added to the verdict. However, the coroner refused to accept this. Mrs. Savill left the court a free woman and the incident was forgotten. The outcome of this inquest was not unusual.

Consider another example. In February 1865 the body of a four month old baby boy, the son of Mary Jane Harris, was found wrapped up in a copy of the *Western Times* on a road in Torquay. Miss Harris had farmed her son out to a Mrs. Winsor for 3 shillings a week and at first had resisted when Mrs. Winsor had offered to dispose of the baby. But when she found it difficult to raise the 3 shillings every week she stood by as Charlotte Winsor smothered the baby. It came out in court that Mrs. Winsor carried out a trade of boarding out illegitimate infants for a few shillings a week –

or the more sinister alternative of putting them away for a fee of between £3 to £5.

The public pressure was growing for some safeguards, although this died down after Mrs. Winsor was sent to prison. But it is an extraordinary fact that by 1870 in London a total of 276 babies, 143 male and 121 female and 12 of sex unknown, were found dead – some in streets, some in alleyways, behind or in dustbins, in the canals, or under the railway arches. As an aside, one of the opiates used to keep babies quiet was called Godfreys cordial and a chemist in a small town in Lincolnshire actually sold 25 and a half gallons of the cordial in one year. Another chemist in the same town had sold 6 imperial pints of the concoction. There was no bar on its sale as it was classified as a patent medicine.

The most famous case of baby farming was that of Mrs. Margaret Waters. There is a hero, one Sergeant Relph who had given evidence at the Select Committee. But before we get to Margaret Waters, there is another much more sinister character, one Mrs. Mary Hall. These two ladies were basically complementary to each other. The following information is from a report by Sergeant Relph:

Mary Hall and her husband David had lived at 6 Chapel Place, Coldharbour Lane, Camberwell, since May 1864, paying a yearly rental of £30 a year. Prior to that date they had lived at 4 Denmark Road, Camberwell, a short distance from Chapel Place. On the door of the house was a brass plate with the name – Mrs. Hall -- engraved on it. The house consisted of 7 rooms besides the kitchen and usual offices. There was a large garden at the rear and a small garden at the front. The house had been a public scandal and a local nuisance for some time. David Hall was more often drunk than sober and his wife Mary, originally a cook, was very stout and repulsive in appearance. She was quite capable of drinking 6 and a half quarterns of brandy before two o'clock in the afternoon. Her husband was a little man whose previous occupation was a carpenter on board ship. Any servant employed by the couple would only stay in their employment for very short periods. The next door neighbour, a Mrs. Warren and her servant Elizabeth Colven, said that many pregnant women were seen at Mrs. Hall's, sometimes five or six at a time. "Much groaning could be heard at night," said Elizabeth Colven, as the head of her bed was against the dividing wall. Also, about once a week and sometimes more often, there was a sickening odour of something being burnt or boiled of a fleshy kind.

This evidence was also confirmed by a Mr. and Mrs. Tennant, who lived at No. 7 Chapel Place, the other side of the Halls, during 1867–68. They had noticed bad smells and had seen Mrs. Hall carry an infant, head hanging downwards, from the house into the garden. They had also seen two small coffins taken away at night, carried by a man. A little woman, a hunchback, used to come, probably after a confinement, because she would take away parcels which had since been traced. David Hall used to do the washing after a confinement, and the tenants had seen him throw lumps out from the cloths to the two cats. Evidence taken from the servants said that there had been at least 46 births in the house. Between 1st January 1868 and when Mrs. Hall had been taken into custody, only eight of those births had been registered. Evidence was taken from a servant, one Matilda Barrett, who had been employed by the Halls from January to March in 1870. Matilda spoke of a baby being thrown down a hole in the garden by Mr. Hall and when examined it was found that the hole was about one foot deep, filled up now with cinder ashes, lime and a quantity of a fatty sort of earth in which there were a large number of maggots. Other babies were taken away soon after confinement. Also in the household were two boys who were fostered there: Harry and Thomas, aged 7 and 6 respectively, whose parents were eventually traced.

There was also the instance of Amelia Woodford from Oxford. Her baby (a male) was born in March 1868 at Chapel Place and two days later he was taken away by Mrs. Hall, who said she had sent him to a good home in Gloucestershire. Amelia Woodford paid Mrs. Hall £20 for putting the child out and £15 for attendance (presumably for her confinement). Mrs. Hall promised the girl she would make arrangements for her to see her baby when she wanted to, but later Mrs. Hall wrote and told Amelia that her baby had died.

Nearly all the women confined at Chapel Place were called Mrs. Somebody or other and were rarely known by their correct names. It was a great point with Mrs. Hall that the servant in her employ should know as little as possible about the comings and goings in the house. One servant, a Mrs. Pullen, who worked there in 1867 for about a year and who actually saw 21 women confined in that time, was becoming, shall we say, a little suspicious. She asked Mrs. Hall where she took the babies she saw her taking out of the house and was told she took them to the Foundling Hospital. Once Mrs. Pullen was sent to the undertaker at Camberwell to order a shawl for a baby that had died. When she became more suspicious and asked further questions she was threatened by Mrs. Hall with an axe.

Another servant, Susan Young, spoke of confinements taking place and women taking away babies. She had heard the name Margaret Waters being mentioned as a woman who took in babies for adoption. It is what Tommy said when the police were digging in the garden which is most chilling. He told them that his father, i.e. David Hall, took babies away and put them in a hole in the garden, pointing out a place near the chicken house, and not only that one place, but others all in the lower part of the garden at a distance from the house of about 20 feet. Anyone digging at the further end of the garden would be clearly seen by the next door houses, but the lower part of the garden was screened by a high fence. Six holes were found, again containing cinders, ashes, lime and a quantity of earth which was wet and slimy and full of maggots. The flagstones in the passage were removed and the closet emptied but no traces of human remains were found there.

Further damming evidence against Mrs. Hall came from a woman called Ann Cummings, alias French, who had left her husband, a railway worker in Fulham. She was now undergoing seven years penal servitude in Millbank Prison. She had come into contact with Mrs. Hall again through an advertisement in the *Daily Telegraph* and she soon became her dupe and accomplice. She alleged that Mrs. Hall used to place advertisements in the newspapers all over England, to take in children and find homes for them. Mrs. Hall would sometimes get £30, £40, or even £50 as a fee, and she would then re-advertise to put the child out for adoption. But she never paid the applicants more than £10 and so she pocketed the difference.

Mary Hall did very well in her trafficking of infant life and running the private lying-in-establishment at 6 Chapel Place.

To illustrate the point about the advertisements the Committee heard more evidence. Another witness, a Mr. Ernest Hart, who as previously mentioned was a surgeon and editor of the *British*

Medical Journal, decided to use a ruse. He actually placed an advertisement in the *Clerkenwell News* – a journal apparently much used for the purpose – and asked for a nurse to take care of a child for a premium. Two advertisements were put in, one for a £5 premium and one for a £10 premium. In answer to the first advertisement, amazingly, he had 330 letters asking if they could look after this mythical child.

Now we come to Margaret Waters. Her apprehension came about as a result of Sergeant Relf being instructed to keep watch on a lying-in establishment and to follow any lady who left there and to see where she went. He followed a lady, who in his opinion had been recently confined. He traced her to her residence and further enquiries led him to learn that the baby had been put out to a woman who advertised in a newspaper. That woman, he ultimately found out, advertised under 27 different names in one newspaper alone. The advertisement in the *Lloyds Weekly* read, 'Adoption a good home with a mother's love and care is offered to respectable persons wishing her child to be entirely adopted. Premium £5 which includes everything, apply by letter only'. And the address given was the Post Office, Brixton.

When the advertisement was followed up the applicant received a letter back stating that a good home would be given. She and her husband had been married several years and not blessed with any children. They would take the child as young as possible so that they would not know any other parents. They lived at Herne Hill but would not give their address in case the applicant changed their mind and wished to claim the child back. When handing over the baby, please bring as many of its own clothes as possible. Later it was found that both Mary Hall and Margaret Waters had sold the clothes or taken them to the pawnshop.

As a result of Sergeant Relf's enquiries Margaret Waters, who was described as a widow aged 35, and Sarah Ellis her sister (a married woman aged 28) were in the dock at the Old Bailey. The proceedings opened on Wednesday 21st September 1870. Waters was charged with the wilful murder of John Walter Cowen, an infant three weeks old, and Ellis with being an accomplice.

It was a peculiar case, said the prosecution, insomuch that it was the system used by the sisters that had caused the death of the child. They took money under the pretence of the care of the baby and that they would bring him up properly and healthily, when the real objective was to get rid of him as soon as possible. And that they would use means for that purpose by which the death was caused or accelerated. After relating the history of how the child Cowen was found, the circumstances under which the prisoners were apprehended were described, and then Waters said that some of the children were adopted, some were kept and others were those placed there on receipt of a weekly stipend.

The first witness, Robert Tassie Cowen, was called. He lived in North Brixton and was a musician. He had a daughter named Jessie Cowen, aged 17 and unmarried. In April he found that she was in the family way and in consequence she went to the house of a midwife in Camberwell Road. The name of Mrs. Barton was on the door. His daughter was confined on the 14th of May. Robert made several attempts to place the baby and he saw an advertisement in the *Lloyds Weekly* newspaper to which he replied, and eventually he met Margaret Waters at Brixton railway station. As a result of this meeting he agreed to meet her three days later at Walworth railway station where the baby Cowen would be handed over.

Police Sergeant Relf, having spoken with Robert Tassie Cowen, wrote a letter to the Prisoner and received a letter back with the usual format, and from this he made an appointment to meet the prisoner to make further arrangements for a baby to be adopted. Sarah Ellis came to the appointment and he promised to bring the baby next evening. They parted and he followed at a distance, seeing her afterwards go into a house, 4 Frederick Terrace, Gordon Row, Brixton. The next day when he returned, he knocked on the door and the Prisoner Ellis opened the door. He asked if she took in children to maintain and she said "No", and asked him what had put that idea into his head. He went into the house, which had five or six rooms, including an attic and a basement below the surface. The house was indifferently furnished and smelt badly. The baby Cowen was produced, who was in a bad way. He went into the back kitchen and removed a shawl and found five infants huddled together on a sofa asleep, with hardly a rag to their backs and those were very dirty, saturated with urine and they smelt very strongly. Two were lying on their backs and appeared to be dying. They were aged 3 to 4 weeks.

When asked if there were any more children Waters said, "Yes, another five in the yard". The Sergeant in his evidence said that he did not know if the yard referred to the basement. There was a phial with the cork out, on the kitchen table, which smelt of laudanum. The children had no names and no means of identification.

There was a baby James who had been given to a Mrs. Rowland to suckle and he rallied for a short time but died ten days later. The other babies were taken to Lambeth workhouse where four of them died. Asked how long she had been doing this, Waters replied four years as a business and that she had had about 40 children. Ellis said, "More" but Waters said, "say 40."

As *The Times* said: The trial opened on Wednesday the 21st of September 1870 at the Central Criminal Court the Old Bailey and Waters (given as a widow aged 35) was charged with the wilful murder of John Walter Cowan an infant aged three weeks and her sister Sarah Ellis (aged 28) was charged as her accomplice but she was acquitted of this charge on Thursday under the direction Lord Chief Baron. The prosecution said that Waters and her sister were engaged in the double business of facilitating the confinement of those women who found it inconvenient of being confined at their own homes and of farming their offspring afterwards, and in other cases by advertisements they used false pretences to obtain possession of children, their object being money. Having got possession of them they treated them in such a way that precluded the possibility of their reaching maturity.

The trial of Margaret Waters lasted just short of three days and the jury were only out for three-quarters of an hour. When asked if they found her guilty or not guilty the foreman of the jury replied, "Guilty." Lord Chief Baron assumed the Black Cap and sentence of death was passed upon her. Her sister Sarah Ellis then pleaded guilty to a misdemeanour for conspiring to obtain money by false pretences in relation to the children mentioned in the trial and she was sentenced to 18 months' hard labour. Sergeant Relf was commended for his part in the case and awarded £20. The High Sheriff of Surrey made the date for the execution as Tuesday 11th October at 9am within the walls of the prison.

Since she was convicted Margaret Waters had become very low and despondent. She was visited by the prison Chaplain the Rev Jessop and also by her two brothers, who on the Monday went to see Lord Chief Baron to plead for a stay of execution. But he refused, saying that there were no grounds for this to be granted. The Rev Jessop came into her cell shortly after 7 o'clock on the Tuesday morning and stayed with her until the end. She prayed until the executioner, Chalcraft, was introduced to her in the cell and it was noted that she composed herself and appeared to have regained the firmness which had characterised her during the trial. After being pinioned and the rope adjusted she said a prayer and shook hands with Jessop, Chalcraft and a prison warder. Death appeared to be almost instantaneous.

William Chalcraft was the longest surviving executioner. He had been born in 1800 and worked from 1829 to 1874. He is estimated to have executed between 400 to 450 persons, including around 35 women. At some of his public hangings there would be between 20,000 to 50,000 spectators. The last public hanging took place in 1868. On the Census returns when he lived in Shoreditch his trade is that of Boot and Shoe Maker. In addition, on the 1851 return is added His Honour the Punisher of the Law, and on the 1871 return he is at Bedford Jail as Public Executioner and presumably he was there for a hanging. He was entitled to the clothes and personal effects and also the rope which could fetch 5s. an inch. It was a much sought-after position and William was noted for his short drop. He retired on a pension of 25s a week provided by the City of London.

It was seen that Margaret Waters had exceptionally fine handwriting and that Mary Hall when arrested had £800 in her possession – a very considerable sum of money at that time. There is also a statement made to Dr. Edmunds by Margaret Waters on 5th October which gives a little more information as to her background. She said she had been settled in Newfoundland with her husband in relatively comfortable circumstances when, in 1864, they had decided to visit England. They went first to Scotland where her husband died in Glasgow. She went back to Newfoundland, settled her affairs, raising £300, returned to England and invested the money in sewing machines to start a business making collars and other items of clothing. Within a year the business was in trouble and she had lost £250. From then on it was a slide into the trade of baby farming which warrants this long story.

Although the law was changed in 1874, and so made the registration of births compulsory, the baby-farming problem still existed and there were other cases. One offender was Amelia Dyer, aged 57, known as the Reading baby farmer, who, in order to dispose of the bodies she had murdered, would wrap them up in brown wrapping paper and then throw them in the Thames. She was only found out because a boatman fished one of these parcels out of the river and the paper had her name and address on the parcel. She came to trial in 1896 and by this time more babies had been found in parcels and the court heard that her trademark was a white tape around the babies' necks. She was sentenced to hang and whilst awaiting execution twice tried to commit suicide but survived to be hung on 10th June 1896. Considering that she had been in business for 15 years, I dread to think how many innocent lives she must have taken.

Her case led in 1897 to an amendment to the Act which allowed local authorities to enter and inspect premises used for lying-in establishments and baby-farming houses. The baby farming continued, however, as in 1900 Amelia Chard-Williams aged 24 was hanged for the crime at Newgate prison. And in 1903 there were the Finchley baby farmers Amelia Sach aged 24 and her helper Annie Walters aged 54, who were both convicted of murder, their trademark being a special type of knot known as the Fisherman's knot.

It also happened overseas, for example, in New Zealand. James Kay was a Railway Guard on the Southland's train service which ran between the small country towns in a daily commuter service. On 2nd May 1895 at Lady Barkly railway siding he noticed a short middle-aged woman dressed respectably in black. She carried a baby in one arm and a black metal hat box in the other. She boarded the train and sat in a first-class compartment. James Kay noticed that when she left the train at Lumsden she only carried the hat box, which she asked a small boy to carry for her for the payment of one penny. The Railway Guard noticed how the boy seemed to struggle with the weight of the hat box. This observation would later be used as evidence in a most notorious criminal case.

The woman's name was Minnie Dean. At her trial, the Crown alleged that Mrs. Dean had administered an overdose of laudanum and then killed the baby. She then put the baby in the hatbox, stayed the night at the Lumsden Station Hotel and travelled the next day to Milburn where she collected another baby, Eva Hornsby, from her grandmother Jane Hornsby. She suffocated that baby, put her in the hat box and returned to her home at Winton where she buried both of them in the garden. She did this for monetary gain.

Oddly, in the eyes of many, including the jury, it was considered that her real crime was not so much that she murdered the babies but that her occupation was both sordid and mercenary and so was an embarrassing indictment of society itself. Minnie Dean was a baby farmer. Her contract with Jane Hornsby was made via discreet and coded newspaper advertisements and letters signed with pseudonyms. However, the advertisements were noticed by an alert police officer who spotted the connection and investigations followed. James Kay the Railway Guard remembered the lady with the hatbox.

Charles and Minnie Dean lived outside Winton in a small, two-roomed cottage. According to the police, it was dilapidated and had a filthy interior, although the garden was beautifully laid out and had a shrubbery. Charles Dean was not at home but Minnie Dean was. She was tight lipped and sullen and denied having seen Mrs. Hornsby or taking a child from her, but a shriek from Mrs. Hornsby silenced her, as a shawl and other pieces of clothing belonging to Eva Hornsby were found. Minnie Dean changed her story slightly but she was arrested and remanded to Milton Court. Later, when the police began digging in the garden three skeletons were discovered wrapped in blankets. One was Eva Hornsby and the other two were identified as Dorothy Carter, the baby in the hatbox, and Willie McPhelie.

The trial was transferred from the Magistrates Court to the Supreme Court in Invercargill and opened on 18th June 1895 in a packed courthouse. Forty witnesses were called during the course of the trial, which lasted until 21st June when the jury took half an hour to find Minnie Dean guilty and she was sentenced to death. On 19th August 1895 she was hanged at Invercargill Goal, the only woman ever to be hanged in New Zealand. During her days in prison she wrote 49 pages of foolscap giving her version of the trial and when the time came for her execution she went calmly to the gallows, protesting her innocence.

Baby farming was both a social evil and a social necessity of the Victorian society. Bastard children were a shame and among the lower classes, an encumbrance. It was the woman who bore the shame, and for the working woman who wished to go on working the only recourse was a baby farmer. The father contributed money and the child was farmed out through a process of legal adoption to a woman who would undertake to care for it and find it a new home. All too often that new home was a grave. Child mortality was high and an unscrupulous baby farmer could kill off her infant charges quite easily. A deliberately poor diet and insanitary conditions would kill off the most healthy child. All too often that new home was a lonely grave.

Chapter 9: Workhouses

The Workhouse is a name that is associated with hardship and the unfeeling care of those no longer able to look after themselves. It was dreaded by many and sometimes referred to as "The Bastille".

My publisher John Spiers's maternal grandfather Edward Everett Root – after which his publishing firm is named – was born in the Workhouse at Hoxton, then the poorest part of East London. Two generations further back, Edward Everett Root's grandmother Mary Eliza Roote and two of her 14 children died there, too. They had suddenly been cast into poverty by the early death of her husband, a journeyman Windsor chairmaker and French polisher. The records of these events survive at the London Metropolitan Archives. He had not known anything of this – it had never been spoken of in the family – until he was led there by a birth certificate entry. As he says, this was a family evidently stigmatized by destitution, and known by local people to be at the bottom. By any measure they were in absolute poverty. The family had been destitute in two of the past three generations, and struggling at the very margins in others. But the shadows of the memories of this grim history, if known, were kept well hidden by their descendants.

So the Street-wise enquirer needs to look at Workhouse records because other significant personal family discoveries might be uncovered! Mary Eliza Roote died as a pauper in the Hoxton Workhouse. She was then an unclaimed pauper, and she may have been dissected, as was permitted under the Anatomy act of 1832. This allowed for an unclaimed body to be sent to a medical school or hospital for dissection. As historian Ruth Richardson has said in *Death, Dissection and the Destitute* (London Routledge and Kegan Paul, 1987), "what had for years been a feared and hated punishment for murder became one for poverty." Richardson says that in the first century after the 1832 Anatomy Act less than half a per cent of bodies for dissection came from anywhere other than institutions which housed the poor.

Workhouses and the background to the establishment of the Workhouse have a long and lengthy history bound up with the Elizabethan Poor Law Act of 1601. This was at first only a temporary Act but it was prolonged in 1603/4 and made permanent in 1640. This then lasted until the New Poor Law Act of 1834. It was very much involved with the many and varied individual Acts of Parliament associated with the care of what can only be described as the underclass of society. Evidence of parochial poor relief can be found as far back as the 15th century. But it was after the decline and then the dissolution of the monasteries in 1536 that the system which had brought people the medieval social structure and charitable care for the poor now slowly moved from the voluntary framework to what became a compulsory tax administered at parish level.

Before the 1834 Act a Parish Workhouse could be a house rented or bought, or it could be a building specially built for the purpose of maintaining the poor.

Sir Edward Knatchbull's Act of 1722/3, which became known as The Workhouse Test Act, allowed that two small parishes could, with the approval of a Justice of the Peace, combine to use the same premises. There was also the thought that the houses should only be entered by necessity and that they should act as a deterrent, so that solely the truly destitute would be admitted. By 1732 there were 700 workhouses, and by 1776/7 almost 2,000 in England and Wales – which equated roughly to one parish in seven having the facility.

One of the most important Acts was Gilbert's Act of 1782 – the Thomas Gilbert Act, the title of which was "For the Better Relief and Employment of the Poor". Its aim was actually to organise parish relief for the poor or poor relief on a county basis. It was to authorise parishes to combine for the purposes of actually setting up a proper Workhouse, but many parishes didn't like this – they continued to act independently when dealing with their poor. By the late 1820s and early 1830s there was increasing disquiet and concern about the way the system was working, and so eventually in 1834 the new Poor Law Amendment Act was passed. This compelled parishes to unite into groupings which would be called Unions. And these Workhouses were for the old, the sick and the infirm, together with children who were without support or who had been orphaned. Any persons capable of working were under no circumstances to be admitted. The first Union that was set up was actually in Abingdon in Berkshire on t1st January 1835. Within four years there were 583 Unions – this was some 95% of the parishes that were actually established.

At the time of Gilbert's Act in 1782 there was a system of relief known as "Speenhamland". This had originated in Speenhamland in Berkshire and it was the chief reason for the discontent with the whole situation in 1782. It was a practice which supplemented the low wages paid to the poor.

That system spread rapidly throughout the country. But it was never satisfactory, and after the 1782 Act Sir William Young introduced yet another Act in 1795 which repealed some of the provisions of an earlier Act in 1722/3 by Sir Edward Knatchbull. This gave the local justices and magistrates the power to grant more outdoor relief by supplementing wages on a scale that varied by the price of bread and the number of children in a family.

You can't please everybody. This in some ways was an unpopular move and probably meant that more parishes were going to set up Gilbert Unions. Their unpopularity was because it was thought for some people that this system made able-bodied men think that they were entitled to relief when they were out of work. And, of course, it could indeed have been idleness. But, too, the margin between relief and low wages was often so small it was hardly worth making a living. And, of course, that is still going on. People may have asked whether it was really worth getting out of bed on a cold morning at 5 o'clock when they were only going to earn £6 more. They may have decided to stay in bed where it was warm until 11 o'clock. It is interesting to think that 200 years earlier this system was being thought about and it still has not yet been very much improved upon.

In 1796 the Utilitarian philosopher and legal reformer Jeremy Bentham had an idea for setting up a national charity company which would in turn create a chain in excess of 200 Workhouses nationwide, financed by investors. Each Workhouse would hold up to 2,000 inmates, who would be fed on farm rations and found work. But he did not find any investors and the idea never actually took off.

During the 1820s there was a growing dissatisfaction with the whole arrangement to look after the poor, the unemployed children, the dependent children, the unemployed, the sick and the aged population. It was felt that the well-represented landowning classes and the ratepayers bore the main cost of the growing poor rate, and they felt that too much was expected of them. From 1815 after the battle of Waterloo when the Napoleonic Wars ended many men were coming back from the war who found that after a short post-war boom there was not very much work. Unemployment rose, and poor harvests meant that the cost of living escalated during the second and third decades of the nineteenth century.

In 1819 there had been an attempt to alleviate the situation when the Sturges Bourne Act was passed. This allowed parishes to appoint a whole committee, or select vestries, to oversee the giving of relief and to help the overseer, which was an unpaid post. He could have a salaried assistant overseer who was appointed. I think that was awfully unfair on the overseer if he was unpaid and got an assistant and they were paid. I don't think I would want to go on being the overseer.

Then in 1830 there were the Swing Riots in the south of England led by a man who called himself "Captain Swing" in a revolt against the high price of bread. Farms were raided and haystacks burnt. Finally, in 1832 the British Government decided to appoint a Royal Commission to review the whole system, under the Chairmanship of the Bishop of London. It looked very, very thoroughly into the state of the poor law administration. It also took account of the work done by two excellent Commissioners – Nassau Senior and Edwin Chadwick, the latter being very prominent for his research when the cholera outbreak in the 1830s and 1849 in London led to so many deaths. It was mainly his work, together with Dr. John Snow and Dr. William Farr, which found the link between the contaminated water supply and this disease.

The Commission took the view that poverty was due to the bad habits of the people. It was laziness. It was a dislike of work. It was large families with too many mouths to feed. It was unmarried mothers. It was employers who purposely kept wages so low that their employees would have to be subsidised from the poor rate, as illustrated by the Speenhamland system. That is what they thought, and eventually the administration of the 1834 new Poor Law Amendment Act was undertaken by the Poor Law Commission. Its Secretary was the aforesaid Edwin Chadwick, who was helped by three commissioners: George Nicholls, John Shaw Le Fevre and Thomas Frankland. The working and implementation of the Act was put into practice with a number of orders and regulations which covered every aspect of the running and the organisation of the Workhouse.

These rules and regulations were supervised by a Board of Guardians for each Union, and these Boards of Guardians replaced the Parish Officers who, prior to 1834, were responsible for the poor and needy. The Board of Guardians and the new Poor Law Union ran from 1834 up until March 1930 when a new Local Government Bill passed the onus to the County and the Borough Councils. A new Public Assistant Committee was made responsible for the destitute. One of the first tasks was to divide some 15,000 parishes in England and Wales into units which were to be known as Poor Law Unions. These were to be run by locally elected Board of Guardians. Local Act Incorporations and Gilbert Unions were to be exempt, and this led to problems for the Commissioners for some time afterwards.

Included was a Bastardy Clause. Acts relating to Bastardy go back a long way. In 1576 there was a right to send parents of illegitimate children to prison. An Act of 1610 said a mother could be sent to prison unless she behaved herself in future. In 1733 the law made the mother say she was pregnant and to give the father's name. The Parish would try to obtain support or maintenance which could be a lump sum or money paid for maintenance over a period of time. If it was possible to arrange a marriage this would be done by the implementation of a Bond of Indemnity usually known as a Bastardy Bond. The Poor Law Amendment Act of 1834 relieved the parish of this responsibility and the Board of Guardians dealt with the matter. Then the mother and child could be taken into the Workhouse and the task of pursuing the putative father would be theirs. The Bastardy clause made it much more difficult to claim maintenance and a mother had to go to the Quarter Sessions rather than the local Petty Sessions and more evidence was need to back up the claim. The Act made the mother responsible for the child until the age or 16 and, if unable to work, to stay in the Workhouse. So unpopular was this Clause that in 1839 the mother was allowed to go to the Petty Sessions and in 1844 the mother was allowed to apply for an order regardless of whether she was on parish relief or not.

Government encouraged and facilitated emigration. But initially Workhouse inmates and those on parish relief were excluded from the programme. In 1833, a year before the passing of the

Poor Law Amendment Act, the Colonial Land and Emigration Commission was set up to supervise a programme of emigration to Canada, Australia and New Zealand. One could put in for a free passage if under 40 years of age, was of good character, could work and had been vaccinated against smallpox. Young married couples with children were considered most suitable. After 1848 the Commission elected that it would allow some Workhouse denizens to emigrate. The Workhouse Orphans scheme was set up in Ireland and many took advantage of the scheme, Quebec being one of the most popular destinations. In 1850 the Poor Law Amendment Act was added to and this then meant that a Poor Law Union could take any poor orphan or deserted child under the age of 16 that was in its care and send them overseas.

In Ireland, following a report by George Nicholls in 1838, there was passed on 31st July that year an Act for the more effectual relief of the destitute poor in Ireland. This was modelled on the one for England and Wales. Unions were to be formed based on the electoral divisions, which in turn were made up of Townlands. By the end of 1841, 130 Irish Unions had been formed. The operation of these Irish Unions was similar to the English ones, with the exception that one third of each local Board was to comprise of unelected ex-officio members, mostly local Justices of the Peace. The 1851 Irish Census was the first to be taken since the Great Famine of 1845. In the wake of the Great Famine, between 1849 and 1853 a further thirty-three Unions were created, mainly in the west of Ireland. This was achieved by subdividing some of the existing Unions as well as some additional boundary adjustments where needed. For example, in County Clare, the northern part of Ennistymon Union was split off to create the Ballyvaughan and Corofin Unions.

In Scotland in January 1843 a Commission of Enquiry was set up to consider the operation of Poor Laws there. The report in 1844 noted that poor relief in Scotland was generally confined to the old, the sick and the mentally ill. Relief to the able-bodied was rare. It was proposed basically to keep the relief organised at the parish level but any parishes particularly in the urban areas should be united for relief purposes, and this would include the establishment of united Workhouses or poorhouses. All this came into force in August 1845. The predominance of outdoor relief at parish level continued but around 70 poorhouses were built and most of these were administered by combinations.

Why did people have to resort to entering a Workhouse? The reasons varied: too old to work, too sick to work, mentally unstable, physically handicapped, orphaned, a widowed mother with several children to bring up – as was the case with my publisher's ancestor – and unmarried mothers abandoned by their family or the father of the baby. After 1834 there was classification of the inmates: Aged or infirm men; Able bodied men and boys over the age of 13; Boys over 7 years of age and under 13; Aged and infirm women; Able bodied women and girls over the age of 16; Girls over the age of 7 and under 16; and Children under the age of 7.

Each category of person had its own area in the Workhouse and husbands and wives, mothers and children could be parted on entrance, although in 1847 this rule was altered to allow married couples over the age of sixty to be together.

The Workhouse itself was virtually self-supporting: there were laundries, bakeries, shoemakers, tailors and areas for growing vegetables. There were also schoolrooms, nurseries, and an infirmary or wards to nurse the sick. There was a mortuary and a chapel. The beds were not comfortable, being narrow and hard, and children often shared a bed. Tramps or vagrants could be admitted for the night. The lavatory arrangements were basic at the least – sometimes shared by as many as a hundred inmates. Dormitories were provided with chamber pots or after 1860 earth closets – boxes with dry soil which could afterwards be used as a fertiliser. The smell can only be imagined, and this would be added to by the fact that the inmates were only bathed once a week and the men were then shaved.

In the Ladies London Asylum there was the substitution of water closets for earth closets. The female ward was attended with great advantage as regards the purity of the air in the ward. The daily routine was strict and unvarying except by the season: from 25th March to 29th of September they got up at 6 and went to bed at 8. Breakfast was from 6.30 – 7.00. Work from 7 – 12. Dinner 1 – 2. Work again from 2 – 6. Supper from 6 – 7. This varied in the winter when they rose at 7; breakfast from 7.30 – 8; work from 8 – 12; dinner from 12 – 1; work from 1 – 6; supper 6 – 7; bed 8 o'clock. A bell sounded to announce the meal times during which silence was observed. The rules were strict and exhibited for all to see. They were read out by the Master or the Governor once a week or once a month so that there could be no excuses made by those unable to read.

After 1834 two types of behaviour could be punished. One more harshly than the other. Firstly there was what was known as Disorderly behaviour. This involved being noisy, swearing, not cooperating or not obeying orders. The second and more serious was Refractory behaviour. This covered being drunk, insulting a member of staff, damaging property or assaulting another person. Workhouse punishment books record what happened to the offenders who swore or were doing their work in a dilatory fashion. Then a diet of bread and water was served, and they were kept locked up for 24 hours. One example concerned quarrelling and fighting, and this particular instance took place between two women. The punishment meant no meat for a week. Another example concerned James Park, who deserted by going over a wall. He was whipped when he was caught. Another, Elizabeth Soaper, swore in the dormitory, attempted to stir up the other inmates to be insubordinate and refused to work. For this she was taken before the magistrate and sent to prison for 14 days' hard labour. The Chairman of the Board of Guardians made a note in the margin which read "Would not have 28 days been better".

Diet was monotonous. At breakfast it was bread or porridge or gruel, both made with water. Meat and potatoes and vegetables at dinner time and bread and cheese at supper or a meat broth. This was made from the water the meat had been boiled in, with a few onions and some root vegetables added and thickened with barley or oatmeal. Sometimes there could be a rice pudding or a plain suet pudding. Beer was allowed and also tea for the older inmates – often without milk. Although the lack of fats and sugar could now be considered healthy, all the ingredients were of poor quality, obtained by the Master at the cheapest price. Food did improve in the latter part of the nineteenth century and in 1901 there was a manual for Workhouse cookery recipes prepared by the National Training School of Cookery.

There were male and female dining halls and the inmates sat in rows all facing the same way. The dining halls often doubled up as a chapel. A pair of scales was available if someone thought their meal was underweight but it would have been almost an act of heroism to take the plate to the scales. As always, the food and the amount could vary from Workhouse to Workhouse, much being dependent of the attitude of the Master or Matron. At one time the diet was considered worse than that for convicts on the hulks awaiting transportation.

We know about the rules for behaviour in the dining room in one Workhouse from a Rule book: That the dishes are washed twice a day or more often by the cooks and the dining room tables be washed every day. That prayers be read in the public dining every morning before breakfast and every evening before supper and that grace be duly said at lunch and supper. That all the poor who attend prayers sit decently at their meals, avoid talking, make no attempt to leave the dining room till thanks are returned and in default in any of these particulars they shall lose their next meal. None of the poor maintained in this house shall carry any bread or cheese or any other provision without leave of the Master, out of the dining room. To avoid any disputes which may arise from telling lies the offender shall by order of the Master be set to stand upon a stool in the dining room during dinner with a paper fixed upon his or her breast whereon shall be written infamous liar and shall lose that meal.

In another Workhouse, the elderly people dined first and if there was any food left on their plates the children came in afterwards and finished it up. It is obvious that standards varied throughout the country and in some Workhouses you might be better and more regularly fed than struggling outside on low wages and with a father who spent his wages before his wife got her housekeeping.

We know about the work done, too. The inmates were given a variety of jobs or work to undertake, most of which was involved in the daily running of the Workhouse. The women mainly did the domestic work: cleaning, helping in the kitchen and in the dairy or in the laundry. Some Workhouses had workshops for sewing, spinning or weaving. One gives a list of the occupations of the inmates which included 18 potato peelers, 22 knitters, 4 stocking darners and 2 looking after the sanitary arrangements. The men worked hard: there was stone breaking (the product was for sale as road-making material). Corn grinding by heavy mill stones which were rotated by four or more men who turned a capstan. The flour produced was usually of a very poor quality. There was gypsum crushing for the use in paste making, and oakum picking and wood chopping. Oakum picking involved teasing out the fibres from old hemp ropes so that they could be sold to the navy or other ship builders. Bone crushing was most unpleasant work as the smell left much to be desired. The rammers which were used to crush the bones were made of iron and weighed 28 pounds and boys as young as eight and ten were employed in the work. The rammers were so heavy that they had to work in pairs.

In 1842 a report found that children in certain Workhouses in South Staffordshire were sending boys, some only eight years old, to work in the coal mines. Their job title was Hurriers and they had to take the corves filled with coal from the coal face to the bottom of the pit shaft for the corves to be hauled to the surface.

Andover Workhouse at that time had as Master Colin McDougal, an ex-Sergeant Major who had fought at Waterloo. He ran Andover, together with his wife Mary Ann, who was described as a violent sort of woman who ran the Workhouse rather like a prison. The inmates had to eat their food with their fingers and unlike some Workhouses – which gave out extra rations at Christmas and on Queen Victoria's birthday – this did not happen at Andover. The Guardians did not visit regularly. Eventually questions about the cruel and inhuman management of the Workhouse were raised in Parliament and the McDougals resigned.

In Huddersfield complaints had been made from about 1843 about conditions there and in 1848 an enquiry found that the inmates were left for nine weeks without a change of bedding, that beds in which they slept and where inmates had died from typhus were used again without having been cleaned. The beds were just bags of straw and shavings, mostly on the floor and which were covered in lice. Often there were two people in the same bed, one person with an infectious disease, and in one case a living man had been left in a bed with a dead man. Overcrowding was rife and children slept four, five, six and once ten in a bed. Despite this revelation, very little was done to relieve the conditions and there was another enquiry in 1857. By 1862 things had started to improve there.

Some Workhouse overseers were surprisingly young. At one Workhouse the master and his wife were only 23 and 18 years of age respectively. It was an occupation often taken up by ex-military personnel. At the Workhouse at Stratford-on-Avon the Master, Daniel Pickett, was there for 33 years. He was a good Master, and that the occupation ran in the family is illustrated by finding that one son Tom was the Master at Pontefract in Yorkshire and his other son was the Assistant Master at Stoke-on-Trent.

Conditions inevitably varied widely. In an 1865 report for one Workhouse it was reported that although the wards were small and badly lit they were quite cheerful as the walls were brightly decorated and had prints hanging on them and in the windows there were some flowerpots. The bedlinen was clean as they were allowed two clean sheets a week. Bed rests were also supplied so any bedridden inmate could be propped up. There were stomach and foot warmers together with shawls for the cold weather. Sore backs were rare, dressings were clean and medicine when needed was given regularly. The nursing in the sick wards was undertaken by the inmates and they were paid one and sixpence a week. However, the labour wards were in poor condition, with the women unkempt, and in dirty bed linen and filthy clothes or nightwear.

There were uniforms for inmates. For many years Workhouse inmates could be marked out by clothing or badges of different colour. At one time in some Workhouses unmarried mothers wore yellow but the Poor Law Commissioners deplored this practice in a note entitled "Ignominious Dress for Unchaste Women in Workhouses".

As to costs, building a Workhouse could be from £3,500 to £8,000. There was a standard design which was usually 'Y' shaped. They were built to accommodate anything from 200 inmates to 500 or 600 inmates, although in Sheffield in the latter half of the nineteenth century it was nearer 2,000. The Board of Guardians who were responsible for the Workhouse generally consisted of about 30 or so members and represented the parishes which fell within the Union. The Workhouse Master with his wife acting as his assistant – sometimes called the Matron – kept the establishment running on a day-to-day basis, with a nurse and sometimes a salaried Chaplin as well. The welfare of the inmates depended heavily on the nature of the Master. In some instances they were harsh disciplinarians determined to keep order and run as tight a ship as possible.

The 1844 Poor Law Act allowed the Poor Law Commissioners, acting through the Local Guard of Guardians, to appoint schoolmasters so that the children could be taught the basics in reading, writing and arithmetic. Unfortunately not every Workhouse complied with the Act. By 1850 there was An Annual Calendar of Certificates for Teachers of Parochial Union Schools. These go by County and Parish, name of the school, Certificate Class and Salary.

The Street-wise enquirer will find that the records relating to the Poor Law Unions and Workhouses fall mainly into two categories. Firstly local, those held at the County Record Office in the locality of the particular Union. And secondly centralised, those deposited in the National Archives, which are now at Kew. If you are lucky you will find some or all of the following:

Board of Guardian Minute Books
Ledgers and Accounts
Admission and Discharge Registers
Orders of Removal
Orders for Medical Relief
Orders for Maintenance under the 1845 Bastardy Act
Registers for baptisms and burials
Indoor Relief granted
Pauper's next of kin
Children under the control of the Guardians
Children boarded out
Bathing Register
Vaccinations

In 1861 there was a Census return of Adult Paupers in each Workhouse. This was continuous for five years, giving inmates' names, and the amount of time each pauper had been in the Workhouse in years and months. The reasons why he or she was unable to work or maintain themselves varied from Imbecile, Lunatic, Orphan or just unable to work. There is a 10 per cent sample on the Genuki website – this was taken by Parliamentary Paper no. 490 in 1861.

On many of the Census returns for the Workhouses people come from other parts of the country. This information is very useful for finding ancestors who have strayed away from their original place of origin. Some of the inmates would appear to have fallen on hard times – a clockmaker, an ironmonger and a retired solicitor have been found, for example. At the other end of the scale were three young children of a transported felon, two children of another transported felon, and two young unmarried mothers put down as prostitutes.

A look at Wolverhampton Workhouse in 1881: Built between 1836 and 1838 at a cost of £9,000 to accommodate 750 inmates, eventually it housed 1,000 inmates. Headed by the Master and the Matron, the staff included a Schoolmaster and two Assistant Masters, two Schoolmistresses, one of whom taught the infants, an Industrial Trainer, Nurses and Attendants for the Infirmary and the Infectious Ward, a Tramp Master and a Tramp Mistress for the Casuals and a Funeral Superintendent. There was an Exercise Yard but the position of the Workhouse was not a healthy one, being on the Bilston Road where the adjacent factories filled the air with smoke. Many of the inmates had something the matter with them, including being Paralytic from Birth, Epileptic, Chronic Mania, Melancholy, Idiot from Birth and Weak Minded.

The 1834 Poor Law Amendment Act made no mention of tramps and vagrants who required overnight accommodation, but by 1837 a compromise had been arrived at and quarters were made available at the Workhouse – usually separate from the main buildings. In the late afternoon a queue would form for admission at five or six in the evening. Leave it too late and there would be no room left. As the doors opened the arrivals would be searched for money, alcohol or tobacco, which was confiscated until the next morning. Those admitted were then undressed, bathed, mostly in water which had been used several times before, and their clothes were taken away to be washed – this was very necessary as fleas and lice were a constant problem. Then they were given a blanket and a Workhouse nightshirt. Supper was next – mainly some sort of gruel, the leftover of which was reheated for breakfast, and some bread. Up early in the morning, they generally worked for a few hours before they were sent on their way.

The 1882 Casual Poor Act made it a requirement to spend two nights in the Workhouse so that a full day's work could be undertaken and then the individual could leave earlier the next morning so that they could get to the next Workhouse in good time for admission there. Prior to the Act it had been found that when they left after a morning's work it would often be impossible to get to the next Workhouse in time for a bed. If you entered the Workhouse on a Saturday you spent an extra day there as no work except that which was essential was allowed on a Sunday. You were not permitted to return to the same Workhouse within 30 days and tramping circuits became established so that this could be avoided. A colloquial term used for the Casual Wards was "The Spike" – thought possibly to originate from the small metal nail used for oakum picking or the large metal nail used for stone breaking.

If they survive there are records from 1850 to 1930 for the Return of Tramps applying for relief. On these are given details of name, where to and from going, complexion, eye colour and particular marks. The applications rose steadily over the years and only dropped during the First World War.

The Street-wise student should search out *The Poor Law Union Gazette*. This advertised details of men who needed to be found as they had deserted their families and were wanted for maintenance. One man was described as a great poacher of game and fish and another as fond of drink and rather quarrelsome.

Fortunately for the searcher, many necessary Workhouse records are now available via the catalogues at County Record Offices. That's where you will find most of them – or in the Record Offices in the big cities.

For Workhouse inmates it was a hard life, but I suppose in some ways it might have been better than outside. However, many people all their lives had a terrible fear of going to the Workhouse, and this really persisted into the twentieth century. Finally after 1913 the use of the word Workhouse was replaced by the term Poor Law Institution in official usage. But the associations with the word continued to live on. The depression which followed the First World War and the General Strike of 1926 put an additional burden on the Workhouses, and in 1928 Neville Chamberlain introduced the Local Government Act whereby the Board of Guardians would be abolished and the responsibility would be handed to the local councils. The Act was passed on 27th March 1929 and came into force on 1st April 1930. Although this was effectively the end of the Workhouse, many institutions carried on as before, and it was not until the National Health Act of 1946 became law on 5th July 1948 that the system finally changed.

There are records of some Workhouse recipes. Soup: per gallon of water 24ozs. of beef to remain in the soup, 14ozs. of split peas, 4ozs. of oatmeal, 16ozs. of potato, 8ozs. of bones and 3ozs. of carrots. Broth: per gallon of meat liquor in which the meat was boiled, 4ozs. of oatmeal. Parsley, pepper and salt also known as "Skilly". Suet pudding: 7ozs. of flour and half an oz. of suet, 2ozs. of skimmed milk and salt. Rice pudding: 3ozs. of rice half an oz. of suet and sugar, salt, spice and water. I like the story of the young boy in the Workhouse in the early twentieth century who said how every Saturday night they were given a cupful of Epsom Salts and you can guess where he spent his Sunday.

There was always a stigma attached to Workhouse births, so after 1904 in Brighton any child that was born in the Workhouse had the address shown as 250 Elm Grove Brighton on their birth certificate. This building became Brighton General Hospital, but locals still referred to it as "the Workhouse" even into the 1970s. There is the story of Penny whose birth certificate in 1943 stated that she was born in the Workhouse in Buckingham. This statement was always greeted with silence as the person addressed was unsure of how to reply. The reason for her being born there was because her mother lived in London and there was a risk of mother and child being a victim of an air raid.

Death registers were kept in the Workhouse: when a person died their relatives were to be informed so they could have the person buried. But, as I said, when there were no relatives or friends a pauper's funeral occurred if there was burial ground within the grounds attached to the Workhouse or in a local cemetery, usually with no mourners. "Rattle his bones over the stones," children would chant behind the workhouse cart heading for the pauper pit, "it's only a pauper whom nobody owns." Thomas Noel's poem 'The Pauper's Drive' (1841) is the source of this refrain.

There was basic medical care. There were vaccinations. I know a record of a baby in the Workhouse whose arm was swollen from its fingers to its elbow afterwards. Sometimes the vaccination was done by an instrument with an ivory point to it. A mother took her baby to a Dr. Chalmers who attended her until the baby died in great agony. At the inquest the verdict was "Death caused by suppurative meningitis following the ulceration of vaccine vestiges on the arm". Vaccination had been made compulsory in 1854 but some parents were very reluctant to have their children vaccinated. Yet there was always the pressure, the summons, the fines or even imprisonment if this was not done.

The most common complaint in or out of the Workhouse, heard by the vaccinators from the mothers was, "no I won't have my baby's arm scratched if I can help it". There was one very sad case again, not actually in the Workhouse, of a Mrs. Clark who kept on putting off the vaccination until it actually happened. She tore up the floorboards in her house and in the cistern underneath she drowned not only herself but her baby as well. So obviously people were terrified of the vaccination. Quite interesting is how much compulsory vaccination there was.

Chapter 10: Lunatic asylums

The Street-wise genealogist will want to examine what happened to those unfortunates who were involved in lunacy – as patients – and to look at those engaged in its management. These included the poor *and* the affluent. For example, two of our greatest novelists, W. M. Thackeray and Edward Bulwer-Lytton, both had their wives incarcerated. Thackeray's wife, Isabella, succumbed to depression after the birth of their third child, in 1840. When he realised the gravity of his wife's condition Isabella was put into professional care, and she deteriorated, ending up in two different asylums in or near Paris until 1845. Then Thackeray took her back to England. Rosina Doyle Wheeler married Edward Bulwer-Lytton but the couple legally separated in 1836. She was consequently placed under restraint as insane, but liberated a few weeks later following a public outcry. As we will see, there were other extraordinary characters involved in the lunatic "business". The records reveal some very distressing and moving personal stories too.

The Poor Law Act of 1601 had only considered help and assistance for the poor and the unemployed. There was no consideration given as to what to do with the insane or those thought to be idiots. So these were left at liberty, providing they were not a danger to anyone. An Act of 1714 stated that it was permissible to put a restraint on the furiously mad and dangerous lunatics, and a further Act of 1744 provided somewhat optimistically for their cure. From then on Madhouses began to develop, taking in lunatics from the more affluent members of society. With few exceptions these were fee-paying institutions. They were the first specialised places for the insane to be housed. Charles and Mary Lamb, the co-authors of Lamb's *Tales from Shakespeare*, both suffered from mental problems, and on 22nd September 1796 Mary, the third child in a family of seven (and so possibly the eldest daughter), was probably in a very emotional stressed state from having to add to their income by sewing all day and looking after her elderly mother all night. She snapped, it was said, when with wild shrieks she turned and stabbed her mother to death with a table knife. At her trial there was no legal status of insanity so the jury returned a verdict of lunacy, thus avoiding a sentence of death.

Charles put her into one of the private madhouses called Fisher

House in Islington, where she remained until her father died, when Charles took her home. And, despite both of them suffering bouts of depression, they wrote *Lamb's Tales* with Charles doing the *Tragedies* and Mary, rather oddly I feel, doing the *Comedies*.

In the eighteenth century hospitals and sometimes wards within a hospital were established by public subscription for patients. But by the end of the eighteenth century, for the less fortunate the Workhouses, the houses of correction and the prisons had a large number of lunatics and idiots mixed in with the other inmates. Something had to be done to alleviate the situation.

On 15th May 1800 James Hadfield attempted to assassinate George III and the ball of his pistol narrowly missed the King. This caused the 1800 Criminal Lunatic Act to be passed, which pointed the way to the safe custody of criminal lunatics. It was their long-term detention which paved the way to The County Asylum Act of 1808. This Act would provide for the building of Mental Hospitals to be built in each English county. Some were to be designed by notable architects and are now listed buildings. It was the first Act which would enable counties to raise the rate to build asylums, and so remove lunatics from prisons and Workhouses to the new asylums where it would be much easier to look after them.

The 1828 County Asylum Act, which was set up by the Home Secretary's Metropolitan Commission, was concerned by the conditions, which included moral behaviour. Also, to ensure the holding of Divine Service. In 1832 this Act was extended to include what employment, recreation and entertainment was provided. This may have been necessary, for in 1830 Dr. Edward Wright was found at night with some female patients – and although he denied any misbehaviour he was sacked after an enquiry was held. Later he went to Syria, a fondness for drink was noticed and he came back to London in 1834 where he did not stay as he left for Australia.

Two of the first County Asylums were built in Bedford and Nottingham, but very little was done by the county authorities to follow these instructions and by 1845 the Lunatics Act had to be enacted to chivvy the other authorities to begin building the institutions required. The Act appointed Commissioners in Lunacy and a Secretary and they were to be full-time paid officers, the Commissioners to get £1500 per annum and the Secretary £800 per annum. There were also five other Commissioners who were honorary. Their job was to visit and inspect conditions in the asylums and also the accommodation, the diet and the care of the inmates. They were also entitled to visit Workhouses and prisons and to make their reports on what they found. How thorough this system was is doubtful because, despite this regime, throughout the nineteenth century overcrowding and staff shortages put heavy pressure on the Asylums. At the end of the century there were 74,000 patients in public asylums.

One example was the West Riding Pauper Lunatic Asylum for the Insane Poor in Yorkshire, opened on 23rd November 1818, being one of the earliest built after the 1808 Act. There are some very detailed records still extant. Originally built to contain 150 patients, by 1900 there were 1,469 in residence.

From the female case-book it is interesting to see that one woman was treated with cannabis and bromide to calm her down and make her easier to manage. Another woman, Sarah Drabble, aged 37, who was admitted in 1832, was the mother of 18 children. Lettice Hodkinson, admitted on 9th June 1824, aged 39, was married and had nine children, the youngest aged six weeks. She had been assessed as insane for 12 months. She was given rice milk and strong butter with rice, and a glass of wine three times a day. Then the wine was stopped and she was given a pint of ale daily. By 18th July her bowels were very loose and during that day she was allowed three glasses of port wine with sago. Next day her bowels were much better. On 6th August she seemed to be getting better and was discharged by request of her husband. It was noted that her mother and her aunt had also been admitted to the Asylum. Treatments included bleeding and purging with leeches, confinement in padded cells and restraints sometimes by the use of straitjackets. Much emphasis (as is seen) was put on the patients' bowel movements, which are given in great detail.

The Bedford Asylum was originally designed to house 65 inmates at a cost of £13,000, but by 1861 it had been enlarged to contain 460 inmates and further extensions to the Asylum gave the building a corridor on the ground floor which was half a mile long.

Colney Hatch – first known as the Middlesex County Paupers Lunatic Asylum – opened in 1851. This was the largest Asylum in Europe and this building actually had six miles of corridors and occupied 14 acres of land. It was supposed to have room for 1,000 inmates but in 1857 and 1859 extensions were needed so that 2,000 could be housed. By the 1880s the Asylum as it grew became very unpopular with the local residents and the words Colney Hatch became a byword for anything odd or irrational. After increasing public pressure the local railway station's name was changed from Colney Hatch to New Southgate. During the 1890s the overcrowding increased so much that wooden huts were erected in the grounds and by 1898 there were 2,500 inmates. Early in 1903 three of the huts caught fire and 51 patients died in the fire. Colney Hatch had its own cemetery but this eventually fell into disuse because it showed that the high mortality rate in the Asylum was unacceptable. Post-mortems in asylums were unusual and rarely carried out – and the cause of death entered on the death certificates was generally vague, such as Exhaustion, Natural Causes and Melancholia.

At one Asylum punishments included being chained to the bed, ordered to bed, put in a dark cell, put in a dark cell and chained up, put in a straight waistcoat.

Causes of insanity were noted as Religion, Religious Mania. One man admitted with this was given "opening medicine" (laxatives) as a cure. Other comments were listed such as disappointment by being left out of a will, violence, alcohol abuse, rage, and lowness of spirits. One woman with this cause was noted to be suicidal and sadly it was her second admission. There was also the wife who was admitted as she was violent and it was stated that her poor husband was quiet and was ruled by his wife. Another woman had been admitted with the reason given as Jealousy because her husband did keep another woman and did bring her home to lie with him.

A description of the Male Ward No 1 at Hanwell in Middlesex which had been opened in 1831: It has bedrooms on both sides of the gallery in the basement with small windows, the longest ward has 50 beds all of whom are occupied by imbeciles or idiots, many are paralysed and helpless. There are four male attendants who keep the ward exceptionally clean and free from smells as each patient has a single sleeping room. Most bad smells are the result of large dormitories, water closets, sinks and urinals. Washing rooms contain six enamelled iron wash basins sunk in a lead top with a watercock and a movable plug. Each patient has a warm bath once a week. Hanwell has 1,000 patients and they use 40,000 gallons of water a day so there is a deep well which they own. There are 97 resident officers and staff.

There were also private establishments where some unscrupulous characters became involved – one of whom was a gentleman named Charles Mott who had previously been a shopkeeper in Lambeth around 1820. At the time he thought he was paying very high rates and decided he could manage the Parish poor at a cheaper cost than the Parish Officials, so he went into business as a contractor to the poor, who he considered were too well looked after anyway. By 1834 (at the time of the introduction of the New Poor Law Act) his system was actually saving the parish £3,000 a year. One of the ways he did this was that when he took over contracting to Lambeth Workhouse he found the scales which weighed out the food were inaccurate as they had accumulated so much dirt and debris that they weighed half an ounce in favour of the inmates. He immediately had the scales adjusted to the half an ounce or possibly nearer an ounce to be in his favour. He had begun to expand his schemes with Peckham House in Surrey which was originally an eighteenth-century mansion in the High Street at Peckham and which was taken over as a lunatic asylum in 1826. In 1829 it was licensed for 172 pauper patients and 40 private patients. Charles Mott's idea was to have a business with at least one other person who would run the establishment. This person or persons would have a stake in the establishment, which would ensure that they managed the place on a tight budget so that they too would prosper. Mott lived in a house close to the asylum and he also had a farm there. At haymaking and harvest time he would use the inmates as additional labour.

With his methods of so successfully cutting the Lambeth Workhouse budget he was able to become in 1834 a member of the Poor Law Commission and was made Assistant Commissioner to Edwin Chadwick.

In May 1838 Mott was sent to investigate the Potato Peeling scandal at Eye in Suffolk where a man was so hungry that he had eaten the peelings. But Mott wriggled out of this by saying that he had eaten them because he was an idiot and not because he was hungry. Later in the year he was sent north to cover Cheshire, Lancashire and West Yorkshire and this was extended in 1839 to include Derbyshire and Staffordshire. By rights Mott should have given up his interest in the Peckham House Asylum in 1834 when he was Assistant Commissioner to the Poor Law Commission but he did not. And until an anonymous tip-off no one on the Commission was aware of his position. In addition, he had caused trouble at Keighley Workhouse where he had insisted that all able-bodied men should be forced to undergo stringent health tests before they could obtain relief. Mott was unpopular and by the end of 1842 he left the Poor Law Commission under a cloud.

But he was by no means finished and in 1844 he was involved with George Coode in setting up Haydock Lodge in South Lancashire as an Asylum. The Lodge had from 1831 to 1841 been used by the government as a barracks for troops and had been unoccupied for the last three years so it was rather dilapidated and run down. George Coode was another extraordinary character, who was born in 1807. He was called to the bar in 1833 when he became a Barrister of the Inner Temple and a year later was made Assistant Secretary to the Poor Law Commission. By 1839 he was made Secretary to the Commission. Both he and Charles Mott – although responsible for Haydock Lodge – aimed to keep their involvement as closed to the authorities as possible as Coode held his position with the Poor Law Commission and should a scandal about the conditions at Haydock Lodge become public knowledge the ramifications were endless and could reach government level.

This became very evident when the building came to be licensed as an Asylum on 17th January 1844. The licence was granted to Miss Louisa Coode, the sister of George. It was for 40 private patients and 160 paupers, and this was upped in July 1844 to 60 private patients and 350 paupers. The paupers came in good numbers but not so many private patients arrived. The plan was to put the private patients in the big house and the pauper inmates in the outhouses, which had been converted for this use. The advertisements for Haydock Lodge were enticing as it was said that it was only one and a half miles from Newton Station which made it very accessible from all parts of the country. The charge was only 7 shillings a week, which was low because of the cheapness of provisions in the area. The large building was set in an attractive situation which was most welcoming for the residents.

However, the reality was that water came through the roof, the gutters overflowed, the drains were defective and as a result rats and mice overran the buildings. The privies were foul and the female yard was full of excrement. There was a shortage of blankets so there was only one to a bed and the heating did not work properly. The peak for admittance of paupers came in November 1845 and during the winter of 1845–46 there were serious problems with diarrhoea and one in four patients died. At one time there were five bodies awaiting burial. During this winter the overcrowding amongst the paupers was high, very probably 75 inmates over the licensed figure which was allowed.

In this terrible winter the Visiting Commissioners came to inspect conditions and they knew that:

1. Haydock Lodge was overcrowded.
2. That there were cases of dysentery and diarrhoea.
3. That water for baths was in short supply, as were the blankets.
4. A patient would have a liquid diet for two days.
5. Many paupers were very ill when they arrived at the Lodge.
6. Large numbers of paupers died.
7. The superintendent did not react quickly or with any enthusiasm for changes to the conditions.

In spite of all this, the Commissioners did not suggest any action until March 1846, when the situation was rapidly becoming a government issue. Six months later in October The Lunacy Commission met. By this time Charles Mott had resigned in May and left George Coode to face the music. Also at this time a Dr. Owen Roberts had been so horrified by the conditions at the Lodge that he had issued a petition to the House of Commons through his M.P. He had also added the fact of the invidious position of George Coode – since as being part of the Poor Law Commission he should not be taking part in the trade of lunatics for profit. It now seems extraordinary that such a clever and intelligent man could be taken in by such a scoundrel as Mott, but so often clever men have little common-sense. And of course, as is so often the case with a crook, Mott still survived. He obtained the post of District Poor Law Auditor which he held until 1851 when he died in Lancashire.

Haydock Lodge surprisingly also survived, hopefully with better conditions for the inmates until it was finally closed in 1869.

As I have said, not all counties obeyed the Act, and certain county authorities dragged their feet about establishing asylums. In Wales the practice was to board out the person with a relative, or if that were not possible then with anyone who would take them in for a weekly allowance. If they could work the allowance would be 1/6 to 2/6 a week, but for anyone who was considered dangerous the allowance could be as high as 7/-. County Asylums were funded out of the rates, thus many counties were reluctant to fund an Asylum and this was the case in Sussex.

It was not until 1854 that they started planning an Asylum and four years later in 1858 it was finally erected and opened on 25th July 1859. Part of the first intake came from Bethnal Green, a very poor and deprived area in London, where an outbreak of cholera found the parish unable to cope with the patients. The accounts for the 1860s make interesting reading, showing what provisions were ordered. They included 24 bottles of whiskey, 89 bottles of gin and brandy, beef and mutton, bread, treacle, tea and coffee and it was surprising to see that there was only 690 pounds of tea to 1,949 pounds of coffee. The patient's clothes were costed: men's leather shoes, women's boots, women's shoes, cloth and canvas boots, men's leather nailed boots – all show that the costing of clothes for the attendants were costed at twice the price of those of the inmates. By 1870 there were 800 patients and they had their own farm, brewery, bakery, laundry, chapel and burial ground. The Asylum – or as it became known, St Francis, closed in November 1995 and the famous yellow brick building has been turned into luxury homes. Thanks to the foresight of the Victorian planners and the architect, it enjoys an enviable position on an elevated site with wonderful views to the South Downs.

From the 1861 Census return we see that the gardener employed at the Asylum lived there with his wife, four children aged between eight and one years old, and with his father-in-law who was a retired farmer. The inmates are only put down by initials, but their age and in some cases occupation plus their place of birth are entered, which can be helpful in identifying your ancestor if one was there. Also included in the papers which survive are Records of Water Treatment. In 1864 patients were packed in a wet sheet for anything from half an hour to seven hours. When it dried out the sheet was renewed. There was also a dry-pack treatment. After being wrapped for half an hour there was a warm bath. The patient was then wrapped in a dry blanket and then six blankets rolled around them. During the treatment the patient was visited every half hour. It took from three to four hours, after which there was another warm bath. The process could then be repeated on medical orders. There seem to have been many orders for two pails of water at bedtime (sometimes in the morning as well), one of 70/80 degrees and one cold. In one case a Roman Bath, which was the subject of an article in the *Journal of Medical Science* in July 1862, was ordered once a week. This was similar to a Turkish bath but obviously this was ineffective as there is a note saying "Did no good".

In the Attendants and Servants Register of 1866 there is given Name, Date of Engagement, Age on Engagement, Previous Occupation or Special Experience. By whom recommended. Wages and allowances. Date on occasion of retirement or dismissal. Here the reasons are of interest and range from illness; to be married; resigned; discharged for wearing patient's boots; to go into business; resigned to better herself; to emigrate; not suitable because insane (and subsequently admitted as a patient); miserable.

Many of the applicants moved from one asylum to another and occupations ranged from bricklayer; soldier; small farmer; shoemaker; dressmaker; needle woman; nursery governess; cook; in prison service; parlour maid; housemaid; kitchen maid; labourer on railway; policeman; engineer. The index gives genealogical clues, with people picked up "from where the applicant came from" and "by whom recommended them" – which is very useful information.

In 1865 the Assistant Medical Officer's Diary notes his extra day and night visits to the ward. The notes give the name of any patient admitted during the day or any discharged or any who died; any serious injury or accident to a patient; the name of any relations written to regarding consequence of severe illness; or, if no relations, any friend. The notes give any observation of the general management and conduct of the wards requiring the notice of the Medical Superintendent. The diary shows that relations like the husbands, wives, father, mother etc. were very anxious to have patients removed from the asylum but more often than not they were advised against this. A description is given of how a Medical Officer reduced a hernia in a woman patient.

Some private patients were admitted. Mrs. Funnel was found

suffering a spasm of the stomach and ordered to drink half an ounce of brandy and 15 drops of chlorodyne every two hours. She had been suffering for some time with embolism of the arteries of her toes of both her feet. Mrs. Denyer was ordered a mustard bath with two glasses of brandy and beef tea during the night. The Assistant Medical Officer visited Mrs. Denyer and found bed sores forming, and so arranged an air bed to be placed under her. Mrs. Denyer was noted as sinking although on the air bed, with sores of a carbuncular nature developing rapidly. He visited her that day at 12, 3 and 5 o'clock. The next day he wrote to Mrs. Denyer's friends informing them that she was sinking. There were extra visits to her at 9.30 am, 12.30 and 5pm, and he ordered a special nurse to sit with her. He called back at 6.20 as the nurse thought she was dead. She had fainted when having her night shift changed. He found her pulseless, but she rallied and he gave orders she was not to be disturbed with having her shift changed. Mrs. Denyer died at 2.30 am the following morning.

After the passing of The Criminal Lunacy Act of 1860, The Bethlehem Royal Hospital, also known as Bethel or Bedlam, had become inadequate. This had first been built on the site that is now covered by Liverpool Street station in the City of London. Instead, Broadmoor – first known as The Broadmoor Asylum for the Criminally Insane, now called the Broadmoor Hospital – was built. On 27th May 1863 it opened its doors at Crowthorne in Berkshire to 95 female patients, and in 1864 male patients were admitted. Its patients included Roderick Maclean, who had attempted to shoot Queen Victoria on Windsor Station in 1882, and 18 year old Edward Oxford who had tried to assassinate the Queen when she was out riding in a carriage with Prince Albert by firing two shots unsuccessfully.

One of the more unusual inmates was Dr. William Chester Minor, a former American Army Officer. He had come to England in 1871 and due to his paranoia, for which he had been previously treated in America, he shot George Merrett, who was on his way to work, because he thought mistakenly that Merrett had broken into his lodgings. This was very hard luck for Merrett, who was totally innocent, the father of six children and with his wife Eliza pregnant with the seventh. Dr. Minor was found not guilty at his trial by reasons of insanity and sent to Broadmoor. As he had an army pension and was thought to be relatively harmless, he lived in quite comfortable conditions. Being a great reader and a scholar, he found through letters that there was a call for volunteers to help with the publication of the *Oxford English Dictionary*. He proved to be a prolific volunteer and was one of the chief contributors. In the end he was so well known that the editor, Dr. James Murray, visited him in Broadmoor and became a friend.

There are valuable statistics provided by the Medical Report for the Central Asylum in 1848/9: Catarrh and Influenza 149, Diarrhoea 60, Rheumatism 50, Pregnant 30, Debility due to Starvation 17.

The Street-wise reader will want to look at relevant sources. One of the best sites to help you find the information is *The Index of Lunatic Asylums and Mental Hospitals* which gives you a description of the institutions and dates, etc. *County Asylums* has a list of counties in England, and it also covers Wales, and although the pages for Scotland and the Colonies are not available, it does have pictures of the Asylums. Then go to the County Record Offices. Some of these sites are very easy to use, but others not so. Hopefully, however, you will find that your record office has a catalogue and you should be able to find what records they have available.

I mentioned earlier that these sources are full of fascinating human stories, both of the unknown and of the famous. One of these is Cary Grant – otherwise Archibald Alexander Leach. The famous film star's mother Elsie was committed to the Lunatic Asylum at Fishponds, Bristol, by his father Elias White in 1911 where she stayed for 20 years. The circumstances and what happened are another story.

11. Hospitals and their records

There is a lot to be found here, in records which survive from the eighteenth century and after. Some of the earliest hospitals which are still used were established then.

The Westminster Hospital in London was set up in 1719 and financed by the bank of Charles Hoare which is also still in existence today, Guy's Hospital was founded in 1730 by a legacy left by Thomas Guy, a wealthy merchant. St. Bartholomew's dates from 1730 and the London Hospital from 1752.

You may be able to find details of family members who worked in a hospital, and also information concerning patients. The Apothecaries Act of 1815 made it compulsory for all medical students to spend at least six months in a hospital as part of their training and I have the records of my own great-grandfather who walked the wards of St. Bartholomew's in the 1850s.

Nursing records can be informative, too. The Nightingale School for Nurses was opened in 1860 by Florence Nightingale, influenced by her experiences of nursing during the Crimean War. She was also responsible for helping to remove the fears felt by many that the hospital was a place in which to die rather than to recover from the illness for which they had been admitted. This was not the first attempt to improve the standard of nursing, for as early as 1840 the Quaker and prison reformer Elizabeth Fry had introduced trained nursing sisters to work in hospitals. Nightingale and Fry both appreciated that one of the biggest problems was basic hygiene, for the germs which spread infection after a successful operation would often lead to death from blood poisoning or septicaemia days or weeks later.

Most hospitals were known until the latter part of the nineteenth century as Voluntary Hospitals, as funding came from public subscription. It is probably helpful for research to outline the different hospitals and what their purpose was.

Admittance to hospital at one time was by recommendation by a financial subscriber. Patients were given a letter by a subscriber to present at the hospital.

It could happen that admittance was limited by the subscription: for instance, one guinea meant one admittance a year; for two guineas two could be admitted.

Pregnant women were not admitted because pregnancy was not an illness but a natural occurrence. Domestic servants, except in the case of broken bones or the need for surgery, were not admitted as any other illness was thought to be the responsibility of their employer. The bar also included those suffering from contagious conditions as they could infect other patients and members of the staff.

There were a variety of different hospitals. Firstly, the general hospital which is sometimes known or still referred to as the Infirmary. Workhouses had an Infirmary as part of the Workhouse, for example, in Shoreditch in East London. There was the Isolation Hospital for contagious diseases such as leprosy or smallpox, which later admitted children with scarlet fever. There were Mental or Psychiatric Hospitals, the Children's Hospitals, the Foundling Hospital, the Lying-In Hospitals, the Lock Hospitals, the Cottage Hospitals and the sanatoriums for TB patients.

Records in most cases are closed for a hundred years, but with the Freedom of Information Act applicants can apply to see records if they are related to the person concerned. There are some excellent records to be found on the internet (which I will come to later), but the majority of the County Record Offices hold records. County Record Offices, of course, are sometimes no longer known as such and there are varied names. For example, the East Sussex Record Office is now known as "The Keep".

In Lincolnshire it is known as the Lincolnshire Archives and this applies to Nottinghamshire as well. Worcestershire is also known as "The Hive" and Dorset as the Dorset History Centre.

What will you find in these records? Admissions and discharge dates, treatment of the illness and the outcome of the treatment and, most importantly, a physical description of the person not often known to the family researcher unless we are lucky enough to have had an ancestor in the army or the navy.

The National Archives, in partnership with the Wellcome Library in Euston Road, London, has a Hospital Records Database. This gives brief details of what has survived and where records can be found. It includes Wales, Scotland and Northern Ireland. If you do not know the name of the hospital you can search by just entering the town.

Here is an explanation of the different hospitals.

A Locks hospital: these were so called as they originally treated those with leprosy and the name is thought to have come from the French word *locques* for rags which sufferers used to cover their sores.

The Lying-In Hospitals were where mothers went for their confinement. One such was the British Lying-In Hospital, a maternity hospital established in London in 1749, being the second such foundation in the capital. The impetus for a dedicated lying-in hospital was dissatisfaction on the part of the governors of the Middlesex Hospital with maternity facilities there. And so a new hospital with 20 beds was established in 1749 in Brownlow Street, Long Acre, Holborn, under the presidency of the 2nd Duke of Portland. It became called the Lying-In Hospital for Married Women. In 1750 there came the establishment of the City of London Lying-In Hospital, and then in 1752 the General Lying-In Hospital (which was later renamed the Queen Charlotte's Hospital). Thus the Holborn hospital changed its name to the British Lying-In Hospital. It moved to a new purpose-built building in nearby Endell Street, in 1849. The hospital was funded by voluntary subscriptions and donations.

Mostly Lying-In Hospitals would only take in married women, but there were some who would extend their care to unmarried women. Endell Street had conditions which said that they were to only accept the wives of poor industrious tradesmen, distressed housekeepers and wives of soldiers and sailors.

Births in hospital, from 1st July 1837 in England and Wales onwards, have been and are registered in the normal way. Similarly, in Scotland from 1st January 1855 and from 1st January 1864 in Ireland. Baptisms were to be recorded by the Hospital Chaplin or within the parish where the birth had taken place.

Mental Health is an important area of researches, and many

sufferers in the recent past were treated in lunatic asylums. A notorious example is Colney Hatch, as mentioned in chapter 9.

Broadmoor Hospital, which opened in 1863, is a high-security psychiatric hospital at Crowthorne in Berkshire, is the best known of the three high-security psychiatric hospitals in England, the other two being Ashworth and Rampton. The records for Broadmoor Hospital/Asylum for the criminally insane are kept at the Berkshire Record Office. With the assistance of the Wellcome Trust some pre-100 year old records are being made available for research.

Great Ormond Street in London is our very famous children's hospital, founded in 1852 with just ten beds. The Historic Hospital Admissions Record Project [shortened to HAARP] at the moment covers four children's hospitals from February 1852, including Great Ormond Street and the Royal Hospital for Sick Children in Glasgow.

Then there is the Foundling Hospital in London, founded in 1739 by the philanthropic sea captain Thomas Coram. This was a children's home for the "education and maintenance of exposed and deserted young children". The word "hospital" was used in a more general sense than it is today, simply indicating the institution's "hospitality" to those less fortunate. The first children were admitted on 25th March 1741. On closing in 1954, 27,000 children had passed through the doors. These records are held at the London Metropolitan Archives. Registers are closed for 110 years, but former pupils and their relatives can get access to these closed records. They contain information such as General Registration, Petitions, Baptism records, Inspection books and apprenticeships registers. Many boys there became soldiers and sailors in the armed forces and many of the girls went into domestic service.

There were also specialist sanatoriums. These were for the treatment of tuberculosis, which was one of the biggest killers. One sanatorium was called the Mundesley, built on the North Norfolk coast in 1899. It was a mile away from the railway station and only approached by two private roads which led to the timbered building set away from the main road so that no dust or pollution would reach the patients. This establishment was only for the wealthy as the cost was five guineas a week and there were extras added to the bill. Fresh air was the basic treatment, but this was most controversial as all classes disliked the idea and there was an exaggerated fear of chills and draughts. Once antibiotics were discovered, sanatoriums were no longer required and they closed down. You should search online for records. For example, the Holloway Sanatorium at Egham in Surrey has the case records for admissions and can be accessed at the Surrey History Centre at Woking.

Many places had their own Cottage Hospital. These started in the 1860s. They were small hospitals run by the local doctors in rural areas. In some cases their records are deposited. For example, in Wales the Abergavenny Victoria Cottage hospital are at the Gwent Archives. The Gloucestershire Record Office holds those for the Tetbury Cottage Hospital and they contain patients' admission records.

Admission records for the Royal Sussex County Hospital show some fascinating stories, such as:

Charles Stevens: admitted for broncho pneumonia but was convalescent at the time of his discharge for wrangling with the under nurse and otherwise creating a disturbance; the under nurse was also discharged by the Matron.

Ephrain Harper: admitted with a sprained ankle discharged for kissing one of the scrubbers.

William Austin: for having a variety of indigestible articles of diet in the ward although previously warned against such a proceeding.

John Smith: for being dressed in the scrubbers' crinoline and causing a disturbance in the ward.

Other examples include:

A girl of fourteen weeks, admitted with a hare-lip. Four days after admittance, the hospital staff performed surgery and ten days after that this patient was released.

Another woman, by the name of Ann King, 50 years of age, tall and spare, healthy looking, from near Upfield, had two children, the last stillborn, some years ago. When discharged, it was recorded that she was a "complaining woman, and made much of her ailments".

A nurse from the fever ward at the hospital who was admitted as a patient. She had been generally fit and healthy, but had been working very hard in the preceding period of time. In the morning, she described herself as "ailing"; by the evening she complained of shivering, pain in the limbs, lassitude, thirst, and a highly coloured urine. She was attended by the other nurses of the fever ward, and made a good recovery.

A patient by the name of Mary Vickers who was 47 years of age, well-made and fair-complexioned. She had imperfect power and sensation in her lower limbs, a condition which had afflicted her for about five years.

She had delivered 11 children, the youngest of which was only 18 months old. One wonders how she was able to have a baby without power or sensation in her lower limbs.

Edward Woodman, 55, who contracted influenza from exposure to the wind when working on the turnpike road. Another patient had an awful cough from exposure to the dust of straws and husks of grain while threshing. The porter at Brighton railway station was admitted with lumbago. He was required to wear a short jacket and every time he bent over, his loins were much exposed.

Thomas Stevens, an old soldier of the 13th Regiment, was brought in on Christmas Day. Twenty years before, in Rangoon, he had received a musket ball in the knee. This wound required the amputation of the limb. He lives on his pension.

Elizabeth Susson, aged 76, was admitted in January – "old woman, half starved, cold, miserable and unhappy, right leg covered in four or five ulcers". Under treatment, she improved and was able to go home.

And there were many cases of women who were worn out from almost constant childbirth who recovered in the hospital, but who expressed the desire to return home to their families as soon as possible.

Another frequent type of admission refers to accidents. Some men were building a railway line. One man was injured by a fall of earth and another fell off a plank.

The County Hospital Committee Minute Book June 1879 to April 1883 gives for Dr Lowdell his record of patients treated. The hospital did have visitors who inspected and toured the hospital daily and on the whole appeared to find everything satisfactory, with very few complaints. There are extra visiting books which record their visits and comments made.

In October there was a grant made from the Society promoting Christian Knowledge for 50 bibles and 50 prayer books. As during that month there were 993 patients in the hospital, there were not enough to go round.

One Monday the hospital was visited by William the Fourth and Queen Adelaide and they went to every ward and enquired with utmost kindness into the welfare of the patients and expressed their approbation of the facilities provided for the relief and comfort of the sick.

The bills paid out during the 1830s by the hospital to the tradesmen and suppliers include those for meat and shin, bread flour, malt hops, oats, straw, to the new gas company for coke, moist sugar, lump sugar, tea, dipped candles, mould candles, butter, rice, vinegar, currants, arrowroot, pearl barley, raisins, pepper, salt, Dutch cheese, brooms and a variety of other items.

There were complaints to a Mr Green, the bread contractor, as his bread was not as good as the sample he gave when tendering for the contract and Mr Acton the meat contractor was told that not only was his meat of an inferior quality but it was not fresh.

Other payments were to staff. For instance, a gratuity to Nurse Batt of 2 guineas in consideration of her long and faithful services, the habitualness of her ward, her frugality and attention to the patients.

The funeral expenses for Nurse Nash of the Chichester Ward were not to exceed 15 guineas, and the cost to include a headstone would be defrayed by the hospital.

Nurses were paid £12 a year.

The wages paid to the staff on the 11th of June 1828 detailed that James Cullen was taken on as a porter at 16 guineas a year with a suit of clothes and he was allowed 2 guineas a year in lieu of tea and sugar. If he left, he had to return the suit of clothes. The assistant porter was to receive 10 guineas, Anne Thompson as a housemaid £8 per year and Mary Wells the laundress £12 a year with the same allowance for tea and sugar. The cook was on £12 a year.

Allowances for beer were two pints a day for nurses and the washerwomen. The cook, the housemaids and the scullery maids were only given one and a half pints a day.

Measles cases were not to be admitted to the hospital as it is an infectious disease and smallpox will not be admitted to the Fever Ward.

Accounts for a Lying Hospital give the names of the midwifes or the sick nurse and for two midwives, in addition to their salary, 12 shillings for fly hire in order to get to the birth. Mostly babies were born at home and at one hospital it was noted that the honorary surgeon's consulting room was only 9ft 6inches square – hardly enough space for the women to lie down to be examined.

For the records for nurses there is an exceptional website of Scarlett Finder, part of which is on Find My Past under Military Nurses 1856 to 1994.

The British Journal of Nursing is online and runs from 1888 to 1956. There is also the Royal College of Nursing Library and Heritage Services.

At the Royal London Hospital Archives and Museums the Archivist is Mr Jonathan Evans and the archives date back to 1740.

The site London Museums of Health and Medicine has a section on Family History which gives the names of the museums and a brief of their holdings. One of the most useful is the Worshipful Society of Apothecaries, as from 1815 they were the medical and examining bodies for the granting of licences for doctors.

Burroughs and Wellcome are responsible for the Wellcome Library which has a very good photographic library with 160,000 images with a considerable collection of information on vaccination.

Silas Mainville Burroughs and Henry Solomon Wellcome were both Americans who they met in England in 1879. On 27th September 1880 they founded in Snow Hill Buildings in London what was to become one of the most successful pharmaceutical companies in the world. It remained at these premises until they were destroyed by bombing in the blitz in 1941.

Silas died from pneumonia in 1895 and Henry from then on was in sole charge. He was a great collector and philanthropist who was eventually knighted. He died in 1936 and under the terms of his will the Wellcome Trust was set up as a research funding charity. The Trust has made many grants for records and archives to be preserved and digitised. Furthermore, in his will Sir Henry specified that funds must be made available for the history of medicine. What can you discover about any unfortunate ancestors?

Chapter 12: Sight unseen. Using the web and sites there

'Sight Unseen' is a familiar expression meaning without seeing or examining something first, without inspection or appraisal of its worth. This expression must without a doubt apply to genealogical websites.

I offer here some specific guidance, although there are now so many websites that it is almost impossible to keep up with what is and what is not on the web. And sometimes it can take a very long time to find the ones which will help and assist you in your research. I give a list of key sites at the end of this book. Some are free but there is a growing tendency for fees to be charged and some can become quite expensive. Here I think of Scotland's People where £7.50 buys you 30 credits or £10 for 40 credits, which disappear at an alarming rate. There is an initial free search. The cost of a birth, marriage or death certificate if ordered is £12 and the photocopy of a Census return is not cheap. The free search includes Wills and Testaments 1513–1901 but costs £5 to view the document and the other free search is for Coats of Arms 1672–1907 and to view is £10.

There are some others I must mention. Among the most important are those of the County Record Offices. Recently there have been some other names given to them, such as the Centre for Kentish Studies or the Northumberland Archive Service. The ease of use does vary from one to another. Mostly they will have catalogues of their holdings which are on the net but the content of the catalogue is not always available online. There are exceptions: for instance, West Sussex has online much of the Poor Law documentation for the county.

Deceased Online was a site set up in July 2008. This has a central database for burial and cremation entries. It has expanded rapidly and is comparatively easy to use. There is a free index search, and then if you want a more detailed entry there is a pay-to-view vouchers system or a yearly subscription – currently of £89. Not every county is as yet included and the date coverage is variable. For example, St Marys Derby is included from 1722 to 1946 but St Thomas Birmingham is only included for 1830–1878. These records are especially useful as our death certificates do not give a place of burial.

Some other specifics: UKBMD. This stands for United Kingdom Birth, Marriage and Deaths. Indexes are based on the original Register Office entries. Some counties have online transcribed indexes for the birth, death and marriages held at the local Register Office. There is also the FreeBMD site, which makes no charge. The recording of births, marriages and deaths was started on 1 July 1837 in the UK. It is one of the most significant resources for genealogical research. FreeBMD is an ongoing charity project, which aims to transcribe the Civil Registration index of births, marriages and deaths for England and Wales, and to provide free internet access to the transcribed records. It is a part of the Free UK Genealogy family, which also includes FreeCEN (Census data) and FreeREG (Parish Registers). The transcribing of the records is carried out by volunteers. The site contains index information for the period 1837–1983, although the whole period has not yet been transcribed. Family History UK is another free UK family tree, genealogy and ancestry community portal website, connecting ancestors and living relatives all over the UK. You can search for your ancestors, and post your "Wanted Names".

The National Archives of Ireland. Here the 1901 and 1911 Census returns are available with some extracts from 1841 and 1851. But the 1861 and 1871 returns were destroyed after the information had been collated. The 1881 and 1891 returns were pulped because of the paper shortage in the First World War. Unfortunately, the 1901 and 1911 returns only give the county of birth and not the actual place where the person was born. There is a free search.

Civil Records of Irish Genealogy can be searched free for Births 1864–1915, for Marriages 1882–1940, and for Deaths 1891–1965. There are plans to extend the site, with Marriages going back to 1845. The period between 1845–1863 gives Protestants' Marriages only. Deaths are given back to 1864. This is an invaluable site which is free. However, many documents were destroyed by fire that consumed the Irish Record Office in Dublin on 30 June 1922 during the Irish Civil War, just hours before the surrender of the anti-Treaty IRA.

The University of Kent Theatre collection at the Templeman Library has a large archive collection connected to every aspect of the theatre in the nineteenth and twentieth centuries which include cast lists, playbills, photographs, programmes and a detailed description of theatres in London and the provinces. It is under Special Collections and is free.

The Anglo-Boer War Museum has a site tracing Anglo-Boer War Ancestors which is very thorough and informative. They are currently compiling a database of casualties. In the British Colonial Service as it was known there were 16,000 Australians and 6,600 New Zealanders serving in the war. Enquiries for searches can be made to vicki@anglo-boer.co.za. There are on Ancestry 54,000 Boer War Casualties which give the name, force, rank, type of casualty, date and place. Other sites that include information are the Imperial War Museum and Forces War Records, which is a paying site.

On the Boer War, Harvey Rawson's Kimberley Diary gives a vivid account of the war and an eyewitness description of the Siege from the 14th of October 1899 to the 15th of February 1900 of Kimberley when the British Garrison was besieged by the Boers.

The Medical Register 1859–1959, which is on Ancestry, gives you the name of the practitioner, the address and the qualifications they have.

The Official *HMS Victory* website gives a history of the ship and what the crew did, and it has The Trafalgar Muster Roll which gives the name, age, birthplace and rank held. The birthplaces come from far and wide. There were Dutch, Norwegian, Maltese, American, Portuguese, Swedish, Indian, Brazilian, West Indian, Jamaican, Italian, and Swiss men, plus Irish, Scottish, Welsh, one from the Isle of Man, English and some unknown. There were the two Twitchett brothers Thomas aged 12 and Robert aged 16, born in England. There were the Rawlinsons father and son Thomas aged 39 and James 14. They too were English. One of the oldest men on the Roll was Walter Burke aged 69, birthplace unknown, a Purser.

The Foundation for East European Family History Studies. Also known as FEEFHS. Most of the maps here have come from one primary source – *The Comprehensive Atlas and Geography of the World,* which was published in Edinburgh in 1882. Most useful are the details of small towns and local boundaries in Central Europe and Russia in the nineteenth century which can be difficult to establish. Fortunately for us, as they are taken from a Scottish source they are labelled in English. Or have been Anglicised or Germanised – which may or may not be helpful, dependent on the needs of the researcher. There are detailed maps for the Austro-Hungarian Empire, the German Empire, the Russian Empire in Europe, and the Russian Empire in Asia and Finland. The list of countries with records available is impressive and includes Austria, Croatia, Lithuania, Montenegro and Slovakia to name just a few. The reproduction is very good. Also on the site are link to selected websites covering a wide range of relevant topics for different European countries, including Estonia, Hungary, Latvia and Belarus.

The Ancestry site contains much, and is regularly expanded. The Prerogative Court of Canterbury wills from 1384 – January 1858 are available on Ancestry and can now be seen free of charge. Parish Registers from the London Metropolitan Archives [LMA] are very useful, especially for the marriage entries as from 1st July 1837 the need to buy a certificate is removed. Marriages which took place in a registry office are not included. The years covered offer baptisms, marriages and burials 1538–1812; marriages and banns 1754–1921; baptisms 1813–1906; deaths and burials 1813–1980.

London School Admission Records 1840–1911 are there, but private schools are not included. You may also wish to see the Electrical Engineers Records 1871–1930; some Railway Employment Records 1833–1963; London Electoral Registers 1832–1965, and British Phone Books 1880–1984. There are also Surrey Admissions to Brookwood and Holloway Mental Hospitals 1867–1900. These give date of admission, name, age, occupation, and the address of the individual (which can be out of the area), their religion and condition.

The Find My Past site – as does Ancestry – covers Civil Registration Parish Registers, Census returns, Migration and other records.

A good site is the London Probate Index 1750–1858, compiled by Dr. David Wright, which covers all London Courts where wills could be proved in that period.

For wills and administration there is now a comprehensive site under probatesearch find a will or probate in England and Wales.

This covers from 11 January 1858 through to the present day. If your search is successful you can then order a copy for £10 which will take up to ten working days to be emailed to you. Soldiers' wills are also included from 1850–1986. There are different systems in Scotland and Northern Ireland. Medway City Ark was made possible by a grant of £49,500 by the Heritage Lottery Fund. This is a free site. Registers cover the parishes which come within the Rochester Archdeaconry area and focus on the Medway towns which are south of the River Thames, such as Gravesend, Chatham and Dartford and certain parishes in North Kent. You click on the list of parishes and find all the churches and dates which they cover. Some are from circa 1568 and some more modern churches from circa 1863.

Dockland Ancestors is a very comprehensive site covering records for those who lived and worked in the area around the River Thames. This is a free database but if you find the entry you want there you have to pay a fee to see the whole entry.

For occupations one of the best sites I have seen is Andy Alston's Repository for a description of occupations in the Cotton Industry such as a Doffer, a Piecer, a Throstle Spinner or a Loomer. I hope there will soon be a similar site for the woollen industry.

Returning to wills, you can see documents on line at the National Archives at Kew. The wills of Royal Naval Seamen in series "ADM 48" has about 20,000 wills from 1786–1882. These give you the name of the deceased, and the date and name of the ship. There is a fee to download them, and this also applies to soldiers' wills.

Victorian prisoner photograph albums for 1872–73 have now been provided on line by the National Archives. Prisoners' photograph albums were created since a photograph of a prisoner made it easier to identify criminals who had been convicted or offenders who went on to commit further crimes. These albums (PCOM 2) contain the photographs and details of prisoners in Wandsworth Prison. Kew also offers some criminal and research guidance online among its many help-lists and guides.

I have included in this book detailed guidance on the Census. Possibly the first Census taken which you can consult is the Doomsday Book, which is at a site called Open Doomsday. Commissioned in 1085, it has a total of 13,418 place names and gives information about the place as regards population, the composition of the households and the resources of the place.

FIBIS covers British Families in India Society. There is a beginner's guide to research in India, East India Companies recruits to India, passengers' arrivals and departures to and from Bengal, Madras and Bombay. Also birth, marriage and death announcements. Find My Past now has the birth, marriages and deaths but Fibis still has a site and now a yearly subscription which includes two journals a year. It is often forgotten how many of our ancestors went to India – and not always returning to the UK but going on to Australia and New Zealand.

The National Archives on their Discovery site give 600,000 service records for Ratings who served in the Royal Navy from 1852 to 1893, year of birth, possibly with date and month of birth, place of birth, ships served on and time served.

Also on Discovery for just two years 1872–73 there are two volumes of the prisoners with photographs. The sentences are harsh. A 57-year-old woman convicted of simple larceny of four shirts and one towel – 2 months' hard labour. A man who stole a whip valued at 8d. – 21 days' hard labour. And a 13-year-old boy who stole a half a sovereign – 21 days' hard labour and 3 years in a reformatory.

The Old Bailey Criminal Court site gives not just the trial of the accused but is also helpful for the other people mentioned. The witnesses are of interest, as are the defending and prosecuting counsel. As above, my great grandfather was a witness in a murder trial.

The sites of charities are important sources. Herbert Fry's *Royal Guide to the London Charities* published in 1917 is a good starting point. The format gives the name of the institution, when founded, and where situated. For example, the National Truss Society; 1786; 2 Grosvenor Mansions, 76 Victoria St., S.W. To enforce and improve the laws for the repression of criminal vice and public immorality, and to check the causes of vice and to protect minors.

The Street-wise enquirer will wish to check what archives survive amongst other charities. They could well have material of interest to you.

The Guild of One Name Studies, also known as the Goons, is a very comprehensive site where you can look to see if your surname is registered. You can see you how many entries there for that name and you can register your interest in the name.

The Commonwealth War Graves Commission site contains 1,700,000 entries. It also includes those killed in air raids, which is very helpful because you can then find the newspaper account of the raid. Just recently, I found the death of a woman who was killed in 1943. This led to finding an administration document for the deceased, which had been taken out by her husband two years later in 1945, and this enabled him to marry the lady he had been living with since 1939.

The many Family History Societies for specific counties have good sites and you will find them helpful if you ask them for information. The umbrella organisation is the Federation of Family History Societies.

For entry into the USA, the Ellis Island Foundation site for a ships' passenger search also includes immigration and crew members. This is a very informative site as to how to search from 1892, now extended to 1957.

Historical Directories are another key source. There is a project undertaken by the University of Leicester which is a digital library of residents and trade directories from 1750 to 1919. This site is now on the University of Leicester special collections online. Directories can also be found on commercial sites.

Gravestones can also be informative. Some major cemeteries have good sites. The very large Brookwood Cemetery in Surrey opened in 1854. Its site has links to the London parishes (there is a list of them) who buried their dead at Brookwood. The site is fee-paying but worth it if you are looking for a London burial. There is a good pocket-edition guide on *London's Cemeteries* by Darren Beach, first published by Metro Publications, London in 2006, and a comprehensive work by Hugh Meller, *Cemeteries. An Illustrated Guide and Gazetteer* (Godstone, Surrey, Gregg International, third edition 1985). There are also individual cemetery guides. For example, the City of Westminster has issued several, including those for Hanwell and Mill Hill Cemeteries. There is also a London Association of Bereavement Services. The Heritage Lottery Fund has recently given a grant to Abney Unearthed, a two-year project to remap the Abney Park cemetery. The Friends of Kensal Green Cemetery publish a number of illustrated guides with maps to burials there since January 1833, including *Kensal Green Cemetery. A Guide*. Also, the more substantial guide book *Their Exits. A Select Alphabetical and Biographical List of Theatrical, Musical and Equestrian Performers and Literary Figures of Note Buried, Cremated or Commemorated at the Cemetery of All Souls at Kensal Green*, by Henry Vivian-Neal. You should google your local area of interest as many new guides are appearing.

You may also have ancestors who were buried overseas. Again, google. For example, the British Association of Cemeteries in South Asia is a charity which helps with leads to Britons, Europeans and Anglo-Indians buried in the Indian subcontinent. See wwwe.basa. org.uk

As to those living abroad, or who had emigrated, an important document is the 379-page *Census of the Empire,* 1901, which was delivered in December 1905 when the Empire covered about a fifth of the globe.

Some warnings along the way. Beware of excessive costs when ordering birth, death and marriage certificates. Ancestry, for instance, charges £22.99. I recommend that you always use the Registrar General site to order certificates which cost £9.25 each. If you know in which area the event took place you can contact the Local Registrar where the fee is sometimes only £9, probably plus postage.

Take care with other people's research. I found a family tree where my great grandfather was stated to have died in London ten years after he had actually died in Jamaica. Errors of transcription are not unusual too – Norwich in Norfolk and Horwich in Lancashire have been mixed up, for instance.

Google anything and everything. You may find local histories have been compiled, a church or a cemetery may have transcribed the burials which took place and have photographs of the gravestones. Try a village and see if they have any family history for the name you are researching. Think of the local newspapers. If you find someone buried by coroner warrant, the warrant could no longer exist but the newspaper may have a report of what happened.

Use Maps and Gazetteers which are vital to setting the scene for finding ancestors. See British History Online for geographical information on counties.

A few other pointers. There are many organisations which can help you. My list of websites offers guidance. *GenealogyInTime Magazine*, online, also regularly ranks the top 100 most popular genealogy websites from around the world. There is also a very helpful article by Charlie Mead, summarising a lecture given to the Society of Genealogists and printed in the East of London Family History Society publication Cockney *Ancestor*, No. 156, Summer 2017, titled 'Putting Family History Online'.

The British Library Humanities Reference Service and Sound & Vision Reference Service online site gives access to many sources. These include the British Record Society *Index Library*; India Office records; family history sources in general; the archives index – the A2A database (now moved to the National Archives site); the Commonwealth War Graves Commission – Debt of honour register; Cyndi's list of genealogy sites; the Family Genealogy and History Internet Education Directory; Family history in the National Archives of Scotland; Family Search – genealogical information from the Church of Jesus Christ of Latter-day Saints; Federation of Family History Societies; Find a Grave; Gazettes online; GENUKI – UK & Ireland genealogy; Guild of One-Name Studies; Institute of Heraldic and Genealogical Studies; The National Archives; Scotland's People – official government source of genealogical data for Scotland; ScotsOrigins; Scottish Emigration Database; and the Society of Genealogists and Society of Genealogists Library Catalogue (SOGCAT).

The Society of Genealogists is the major British organisation in this field. It publishes many individual guides to specific topics, and also the *Genealogists' Magazine*.

Many individual societies are concerned with particular areas of the country. These all publish invaluable magazines and bulletins. For example, the East of London Family History Society issues *Cockney Ancestor*. Like many of these societies, it has branch representatives covering parts of its area. These societies all arrange regular member meetings and special events. There are also many local authorities which publish helpful material. For example, The Friends of Hackney Archives issue *The Hackney*

Terrier. archives@Hackney.gov.uk

The National Archives at Kew also provides many detailed free guides to topics, and is also a book publisher in this field.

Among magazines and online sources are *Genealogy In Time Magazine; Eastman's Online Newsletter; Genealogy Magazine;* and Lineages.co.uk. Genealogy Roots Blog lists new online genealogy resources for US researchers.

There are also many online forums, some of which I list in my website list. Rootsweb is one of the oldest. It is now part of Ancestry.

High street shops (and most public libraries) stock essential monthly guides to current work and news, including *Your Family Tree Magazine, Family Chronicle,* the *Who Do You Think You are?* magazine, and *Your Family History. History Today* and the BBC *History Magazine* are two other popular periodicals which publish valuable material of interest to family historians. Some county libraries offer some of these as down-loads. There are also many academic journals and individual magazines concerned with particular subject areas. These include the *Labour History Review* (published by Liverpool University Press for the Society for the Study of Labour History), the *Journal of Liberal History* (published by the Liberal Democrat History Group), and the academic journals *Family and Community History,* the *Journal of Family History,* and *The History of the Family.* The Institute of Historical Research in Senate House, London has these and several dozen other current academic journals on open shelves. http://www.history.ac.uk/

There is much on offer for Military History. The Commonwealth War Graves Commission has an invaluable website, as mentioned above. Then there are the specialist societies. Those concerned with the Great War will want particularly to see The Western Front Association *Bulletin,* published in March, August and November each year. As I show, County Record Offices will help everyone. There are other museums which will do so too. For example, the In Flanders Museum at Ypres, which is also a publisher. Those with relatives who served their country have many possible sites to see. One such is that of The Society for Army Historical Research.

The professional British associations for historians include the Institute of Historical Research at Senate House, University of London. It issues a magazine, *Past and Future*. The British Association for Local History publishes the quarterly *The Local Historian* and also *Local History News*. It also issues a work entitled *Internet Sites for Local Historians. A Directory*, compiled by Jacquelene Filmore and edited by Alan G. Crosby, and other general publications. The Society journals give links to many local history societies. See www.balh.org.uk.

There are also many county-based local history societies. For example, the East Yorkshire Local History Society, which – like many – issues a regular newsletter. The Society for Lincolnshire History & Archaeology issues *Lincolnshire Past and Present*, which has included a series of reports on local individuals who fought in the Great War. Kent Archaeological Society issues a magazine, titled *KAS*. Researchers will find its account of parishes and their histories very helpful. The commercial firm of Routledge (now part of the Taylor & Francis group) publishes *English Historical Documents Online*, available to library users. The digital revolution expands opportunities almost daily. For example, if you have an interest in the Whitechapel area of East London the *Survey of London* has launched an interactive website, inviting anyone with an interest in or experiences of Whitechapel to participate. It is collecting memories, photographs, drawings and film. The Survey, of course, has published more than 50 volumes of detailed studies of London. See http://surveyoflondon.org

For those who want to try to reach back to the Medieval period the Canterbury and York Society has published some 100 volumes, including episcopal records in printed editions. The society's work has extended beyond the Bishops' Registers, and in recent years they have published a collection of the wills (and related documents) of English and Welsh Bishops. Material is published in English summary, with full transcripts of significant documents in addition. You may be very lucky! See www.boydellandbrewer.com

The publications of County Record Societies are an essential source. For example, the Staffordshire Record Society has issued nearly 100 volumes of records held in national and local archives as well as some general histories. County Councils make available online reference libraries with access to Ancestry, Find My Past, the *Dictionary of National Biography,* the *Encyclopaedia Britannica,* the European Newsstream (for current and past newspaper articles), the *Illustrated London News,* the John Johnson collection (housed in the Bodleian Library at Oxford), the *London Gazette, The Times* Digital Archive (covering 1785–2011), *Who's Who* and *Who Was Who,* &c. *Who's Who* has been issued annually since 1849, and its cumulative volumes of those who have passed on offer 100,000 entries from all eleven volumes of *Who Was Who.*

The Victorian Society issues *The Victorian. The London Journal* embraces all aspects of metropolitan society. The University of the Third Age offers local history and genealogical member's research groups. Your own online searches will reveal other organisations which meet your interests and needs. The Scottish Records Association issues *Retour,* its newsletter, which invaluably surveys archives and accessions.

The Institute of Historical Research in Senate House, The University of London offers regular events, including The London History Day School. It offers British History Online at british-history@sas.ac.uk. It publishes a regular bibliographic update and it also publishes *Past and Future* which reports on historical research news. It is well worth regularly checking forthcoming events at the Institute since the invaluable programme covers many topics of interest to all historians. See www.history.ac.uk/ events. The Institute's library collection guides can be seen at www.history.ac.uk/library/collections and the History Online: bibliographic update www.history.ac.uk/history-online. For London history in particular you should check the Centre for Metropolitan History News at www.history.ac.uk/cmh

Individual trades can be traced on relevant special sites. For example, was one of your ancestors a furniture maker? See the site of British and Irish Furniture Makers Online (BIFMO). The Institute of Historical Research, in nearing the end of Phase I of this research project, has published this database online. BIFMO is a long-term project in its earliest stages and constantly evolving. Although currently the database does not include information on Scottish, Welsh and Irish furniture makers, these tradesmen/ women and artisans will be incorporated into the database as the project progresses. The date parameters will be expanded to run from 1600 to the present day. The Furniture History Society is actively raising funds for this work, in partnership with the

University of Kent. The project is featured in the July issue of the 'Burlington Magazine': http://www.burlington.org.uk/archive/editorial/furniture-history-the-digital-future.

Library sites everywhere offer many good links, both locally and internationally. For example, the invaluable site of the National Library of Australia in Canberra lists more than 260 sites and e-resources, including British sites. The library also has a unique collection of maps which are important to family historians: www.nla.gov.au/app/eresources/list/freeery.

By the time you read this many other sites will have come on line. Some will have been updated and some renamed. So it is worth checking frequently to see if they would be helpful in your research.

The *Really Useful* Leaflet published by the Federation of Family History Societies has a list of 50 sites, on which I have drawn. You should check the family history magazines regularly, for current reports. It is also well worthwhile to subscribe to library newsletters online to stay up to date with their resources for family history.

The Federation of Family History Societies in Australia has published an updated 'Our Australasian Really Useful Information Leaflet'. You can download this free at http://www.ffhs.org.uk/tips/RUL-AUS-2017-0809.pdf. The FFHS has produced this in association with the Society of Australian Genealogists and the Australasian Federation of Family History Organisations. The leaflet gives a long list of websites, and links to relevant societies.

The military records website *Fold3* now has over 600,000 records of early RAF personnel available, 1918-1940. *Fold3* is owned by Ancestry. They are also scanning and digitising World War 1 soldiers' pension record cards. There are some 8 million records. The Western Front Association's *Bulletin* 109, November/December 2017, pp.31, included an illustrated report on progress to that date. The WFA has also established a weekly audio podcast called 'Mentioned in Dispatches', hosted by Tom Thorpe. Contact press@westernfrontassocation.com

Chapter 13: Key Websites

Most of these websites are free to access. The sites that charge to view some or all of their records are highlighted with a £ symbol.

• 192.com: People-finder site (pay-per-view), including a comprehensive database of current UK residents. www.192.com/people £

• Abney Park Cemetery Trust, founded after the cemetery company went bankrupt in 1972. www.abney-park.org.uk

• Adoption Search Reunion: First port of call for anyone searching for, or making contact with, birth and adopted relatives, or researching an adoption that took place in the UK. www.adoptionsearchreunion.org.uk

• AIM25: Provides access to collection-level descriptions of the archives of over 100 higher-education institutions, learned societies, cultural organisations and livery companies within the Greater London area. www.aim25.ac.uk

• Ancestry: Over 1 billion searchable UK records, including Censuses; birth, marriage and death records; passenger lists; phone books, military and parish records plus Ancestry DNA service. www.ancestry.co.uk £

• Archives Hub: Descriptions of archives in over 250 UK universities and colleges; name search facility. www.archiveshub.ac.uk

• Archives Network Wales: Information about more than 7,000 collections of historical records in the holdings of 21 archives in Wales. www.archivesnetworkwales.info

• Army Museums Ogilby Trust: Details of regimental museums. www.armymuseums.org.uk

• Blind Veterans UK (Formerly St Dunstan's): Holds details of veterans' military service; enquiries by email. www.blindveterans.org.uk

• Borthwick Institute for Archives: Holds a large number of archives of regional, national and international importance. www. york.ac.uk/borthwick

• The British Association for Local History. www.balh.org.uk.

• British History Online: Digital library of primary and secondary sources for the history of Britain and Ireland, with a primary focus on the period between 1300 and 1800. www.british-history.ac.uk

• British Library: Catalogue of over 12 million books, serials, printed music and maps; newspaper catalogue of over 52,000 newspaper and periodical titles; India Office Select Materials. www.bl.uk

• Burlington Magazine. http://www.burlington.org.uk/archive/editorial/furniture-history-the-digital-future.

• Caribbean Roll of Honour: Whilst incomplete, a useful website for those researching Caribbean service personnel.www. caribbeanrollofhonour-ww1-ww2.yolasite.com/

• Children's Homes: The institutions that became home for Britain's children and young people. www.childrenshomes.org. uk

• Clergy of the Church of England Database: References to the careers of Anglican clergy from 1540 to 1835; approximately 155,000 clergymen appear. theclergydatabase.org.uk

• Commonwealth War Graves Commission: Debt of Honour Register of Commonwealth forces who died in WWI or WWII. www.cwgc.org

• Connected Histories: Currently includes 25 major digital resources for the period 1500–1900 and allows searching of names, places and dates.www.connectedhistories.org

• Cyndi's List: Long-established genealogical research portal. www.cyndislist.com

• Deceased Online: UK burial and cremation records www. deceasedonline.com £

• Ellis Island: Searchable database and copies of passenger manifests of ships arriving at Ellis Island from 1892–1924. www. ellisislandrecords.org

• Faces of the First World War: Photographs of men who served in WW1. www.flickr.com/photos/imperialwarmuseum/sets/

• FamilySearch: The Church of Jesus Christ of Latter-Day Saints' baptism, marriage and burials index; Census; Family History Centres and more. www.familysearch.com

• Federation of Family History Societies: Long-established genealogy charity that supports ancestry research and family- history societies around the world; bimonthly newsletter.
Recent editions have included special issues on Irish family history, emigration and one-place studies.
Read them at http://www.ffhs.org.uk/ezine/intro.php
Subscribe now at http://www.ffhs.org.uk/ezine/subscribe15.php
www.ffhs.org.uk

• Find a Grave: Searchable database of graves. www.findagrave. com

• Findmypast.co.uk: Comprehensive collection of UK family-history and military records; Irish, US, Australian and NZ records, plus 1939 Register. www.findmypast.co.uk £

• Forces War Records: Military genealogy resources. Over 7 million individuals' research plus supplementary military data. www.forces-war-records.co.uk £

• FreeBMD: Search birth, marriage and death GRO index for England and Wales. www.freebmd.org.uk

• FreeCEN: Search UK Census data. www.freecen.org.uk

• FreeREG: Indexes transcribed from millions of parish and non-conformist registers of England, Scotland and Wales. freereg2. freereg.org.uk

• Gazetteer of British Place Names: Place Name Index to Great Britain. www.gazetteer.co.uk

• Geneabloggers: Genealogy-related blogs. www.geneabloggers. com

• Genealogy in Time: Online magazine and website with search facility, news and newsletter. www.genealogyintime.com

• General Register Office (GRO): Order birth, marriage and death certificates online for a fee; search birth and death indexes for free, which are newly updated with age at death and mothers' maiden name; official site. www.gro.gov.uk/gro/content/ certificates/ £

• Genes Reunited: Online family-tree-linking website; Census; birth, marriage and death entries from GRO; indexes 1837–2004; military records; passenger lists; parish records. www. genesreunited.co.uk £

• GENUKI: Virtual reference library of genealogical information of particular relevance to the UK and Ireland; forthcoming genealogical events on GENEVA. www.genuki.org.uk

• Guildhall Library: Holds a variety of genealogy resources relating to London and beyond. www.cityoflondon.gov.uk/things-to-do/london-metropolitan-archives/visitor-information/pages/ archives-guildhall-library.aspx

• Guild of One-name Studies: Various online indexes, including marriage and probate. one-name.org/the-guild-indexes/

• Historical Directories of England and Wales: A digital library of local and trade directories 1750–1919. cdm16445.contentdm.oclc. org/cdm/landingpage/collection/p16445coll4

• Imperial War Museum: WWI/WWII collections. www.iwm. org.uk/collections

• The Institute of Historical Research, Senate House, The University of London, offers British History Online at british-history@sas.ac.uk. On events www.history.ac.uk/events. On the Institute's library www.history.ac.uk/library/collections. For the History Online: bibliographic update www.history.ac.uk/ history-online. For London history in particular see the Centre for Metropolitan History News at www.history.ac.uk/cmh

• London Metropolitan Archives: Includes Middlesex. willswww. cityoflondon.gov.uk/things-to-do/london-metropolitan-archives/Pages/default.aspx

• Lost Cousins: Matches you with others researching the same ancestors. www.lostcousins.com

• Maritime Memorial Trust: Dedicated to all who lost their lives at sea during the conflicts of the 20th century; merchant navy, naval, army and civilian records. www.maritimememorialtrust.com/

• Measuring Worth: Valuations of British money, from 1270 to present. www.measuringworth.com/ppoweruk/

• Military Service Records: How to obtain more recent service records, including personnel who served in WW2. www.gov.uk/get-copy-military-service-records

• MyHeritage.com: Build your family tree; search millions of international records. www.myheritage.com

• National Archives of Ireland: Census 1901 and 1911; limited Census survivals 1821–51; Census search forms 1841–51; tithe applotment books 1823–1837; soldiers' wills 1914–1917; calendars of wills and administrations 1858–1922. www.genealogy.nationalarchives.ie/

• National Library of Australia in Canberra lists more than 260 sites and e-resources, including British sites. The library also has a unique collection of maps which are important to family historians: www.nla.gov.au/app/eresources/list/freeery.

• National Library of Ireland: Online searchable catalogue, including books and periodicals, photographs, prints, drawings, manuscripts and newspapers; plus online images of Catholic Parish Registers. www.nli.ie

• National Library of Scotland: Scotland's only legal deposit library; main catalogue of over 3 million records plus Scots Abroad database. www.nls.uk

• National Maritime Museum: Over 1.5 million items relating to seafaring, navigation, astronomy and time measurement. Many available to view online. www.rmg.co.uk/discover/researchers

• National Railway Museum: WW1 resources and exhibition; free searchable database of over 20,000 railway employees. www. nrm.org.uk/RailwayStories/worldwarone.aspx

• National Records of Scotland: Research guides plus relevant links; also see Scotland's People. www.nrscotland.gov.uk/research/family-history

• Naval & Naval-History.net: Royal Navy Log Books of the WW1 era; ship histories; WW1 casualty list information; Royal Navy despatches; Royal Navy honours and gallantry awards. www. naval-history.net/#ww1

• Naval Biographical Database: People, places, ships, organisations and events associated with the Royal Navy since 1660. www.navylist.org

• Old Bailey: Proceedings at the Old Bailey 1674–1913; nearly 200,000 London criminal trial records. www.oldbaileyonline.org

• Old Maps: Historical map archive covering England, Wales and Scotland. www.old-maps.co.uk

• Pharos Teaching & Tutoring: Specialists in online courses in genealogy and family history. www.pharostutors.com

• Prisoners of the First World War: International Red Cross Archives; index cards of 5 million servicemen and civilians who were captured in WW1 and sent to detention camps. grandeguerre. icrc.org/

• Probate: Access to post-1858 England and Wales wills; index of wills for soldiers who died on active service from 1860–1982. www.gov.uk/search-will-probate

• *The Survey of London.* More than 50 volumes of detailed studies of London. http://surveyoflondon.org

***

Front cover illustration:

Summer Night © *Joy Laforme courtesy of Yellow House Art License.*

CPSIA information can be obtained
at www.ICGtesting.com
Printed in the USA
BVHW04s2021250918
528488BV00008B/89/P